The Layout Book

Ambrose/Harris

ava | Academia
the environment of learning

The Hard Sell (below)
Pictured is a spread created by design studio SEA
Design for *The Hard Sell*, a book on advertising
photographs by Rankin. The layout makes use of a
full-bleed photograph running over both pages to
provide a simple, faithful, full-size reproduction of
the image with no interference. The gutter is used to
add an element of tension by dividing the image
into active (verso) and passive (recto) parts. In this
instance the book is treated more as a 'canvas' than
a 'page'.

An AVA Book
Published by AVA Publishing SA
Rue des Fontenailles 16
Case Postale
1000 Lausanne 6
Switzerland
Tel: +41 786 005 109
Email: enquiries@avabooks.ch

Distributed by Thames & Hudson (ex-North America)
181a High Holborn
London WC1V 7QX
United Kingdom
Tel: +44 20 7845 5000
Fax: +44 20 7845 5055
Email: sales@thameshudson.co.uk
www.thamesandhudson.com

Distributed in the USA and Canada by:
Watson-Guptill Publications
770 Broadway
New York, NY 10003
Fax: +1 646 654 5487
Email: info@watsonguptill.com
www.watsonguptill.com

English Language Support Office
AVA Publishing (UK) Ltd.
Tel: +44 1903 204 455
Email: enquiries@avabooks.co.uk

Copyright © AVA Publishing SA 2007

ISBN 2-940373-53-1 and 978-2-940373-53-6

10 9 8 7 6 5 4 3 2 1

Design by Gavin Ambrose
www.gavinambrose.co.uk

Production by
AVA Book Production Pte. Ltd., Singapore
Tel: +65 6334 8173
Fax: +65 6259 9830
Email: production@avabooks.com.sg

Contents

This book brings together examples of layout, both contemporary and historic, from around the world. It contains examples from leading graphic designers to provide a sample of the rich and diverse possibilities for the creative use of layout.

beyon™ Storage

The beyon storage system incorporates comprehensive and sophisticated mobile and non-mobile storage solutions for the contemporary workplace. Answering the needs of today's fast moving office, beyon storage consists of 18 personal storage products and 72 Bulk storage products.

Beyon's personal storage includes a range of mobile tambour pedestals with drawers for stationery, hanging files and personal items. Also available in the personal storage range are a series of long, low return storage units offering the user an additional work surface and up to three file drawers or three open shelves for lever arch files both foolscap, A4 and stationery.

Bulk storage units incorporate drawers for hanging files, stationery and CDs, flipper doors with shelving for lever arch files and cupboards with shelves.

The Metal storage units have an optional cable management panel on the back of the unit to allow cables to be passed from the floor to the top of the unit for printers, fax machines and other office hardware.

Beyon (above)

This is a brochure for furniture company beyon created by design studio SEA Design that features an outsize format with a wide measure, as can be seen by the scale of the pencil. The wide measure is analogous to the spacious storage units produced by the company and is complemented with text presented in a large enough typesize to produce a comfortable measure. This sense of scale is counterbalanced by the delicate folios on the verso page.

Introduction

This book aims to explore layout in its broadest sense by looking at examples of the many facets it encompasses from everyday life, in addition to graphic design commercial practice to show how the essential tenets can be used. Cross-fertilisation is central to this book, as looking outside of what we know and are familiar with provides a key source of inspiration and ideas that can be applied to graphic design.

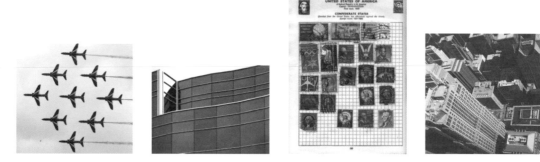

Layout in practice (above)

It is human nature to impose the will of mankind over its surroundings, to organise and arrange things according to its taste and needs, from written texts, the diamond formation of the Red Arrows display team, architecture, stamps in a philatelist's album or city planning as pictured above.

When we talk of 'layout' we think of the objects, images and typography – the familiar elements of graphic design – that a designer positions on a page. Although graphic design is a young industry, many of the principles it embraces were discovered in ancient times and were rediscovered during the Renaissance.

We are familiar with a printed page, building façades, posters and film format, but behind these diverse design-rich sectors are key principles that have been in existence for centuries. The principles will outlast the technological developments and limitations that designers currently face and will be used by future generations.

This book is concerned with the overriding principles that guide layout and the context within which these principles were formulated, rather than providing a dogmatic history of technological development and its impact on layout. Focus will be placed on specific pertinent examples, such as page size selection and creating harmonious balance, as well as the role layout has to play in helping to organise our ever more complex lives.

Concepts from several disciplines will be incorporated into this volume so that artists, new media developers, print designers et al. can communicate their needs, concerns, solutions and ideas to one another. In the spirit of the Renaissance, there is much to be discovered in the familiar and the unfamiliar in equal measure, and the practical demands of different disciplines find common currency in the current zeitgeist that balances the need for experimentation with commercial practicalities. Designers aspire to improve and find better solutions to age-old problems and new challenges alike. Many of the answers lie in a study of the past and the basic principles that previous generations have discovered.

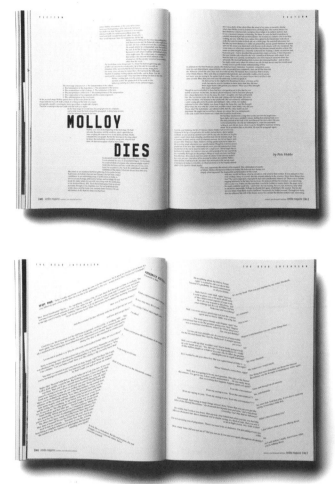

Acorn (above)
This bespoke text design was created by design studio Studio Output for conceptual textiles company Acorn and features a uniquely styled majuscule A (for Acorn) that is richly adorned with a floral motif, which reflects the fabrics produced by the company.

Zembla (above right)
These spreads were produced by design studio Frost Design for *Zembla* magazine. The design challenges our concept of the text column. Typically we think of it as something solid, sturdy and ordered, but these text columns are anything but that.

In an increasingly pluralistic world, the pursuit of standards and canons has not diminished and many of these will be addressed in the final reference section of this volume.

With free-flowing information, the world is more democratic than ever, with people exposed to vast quantities of information and cultural diversity. Design is no exception, which means that there is more diversity and experimentation, but equally more expectation from the familiar. Technological advancement means that graphic design is no longer a mysterious discipline, but something that touches us all. This raises questions such as: Why do people respond to one layout and not another? Or why does one typographical element appear more comfortable than another?

The challenges facing designers will not be met by repeating the present or copying the past, but an understanding of the principles discussed in this volume will equip a designer with knowledge that will prove invaluable throughout their career. Just over 20 years ago few people had heard of the embryonic Internet, but as we enter an age of streamlined digital media, fundamental changes in the way we work, live and consume media continue to occur. What will the next 20, ten or even five years bring, and more importantly, what will we bring to them?

How to Get the Most Out of This Book

This book introduces different aspects of layout via dedicated chapters for each topic. Each chapter provides numerous examples of creative layout use from leading contemporary design studios. These are annotated to explain the reasons behind the design choices made.

Chapter openers
Each chapter has a brief overview and a 'preview' panel (see below). Each chapter opener has a block colour background, making the distinction between chapters clear.

Navigation
Page numbers appear top right on all pages, making referencing from the contents page and the index easier.

Chapter 4 / Objects on a Page

How an object is placed on a page has a dramatic impact on how it is received and interpreted by the viewer, and the message that it delivers. We have looked at how grids can be used to guide element placement on a page, but maintaining a sense of order is not the only consideration when laying out a design.

Object placement helps form the narrative of a design and is constructed from an understanding of how we read a page. The narrative of a design can be created and altered by a wide range of placement and intervention strategies, such as how white space is used, the balance and relative weight given to other objects, the juxtaposition or contrast of objects and so on.

This chapter will outline some of the fundamental approaches to object placement.

Fictional (opposite)
This is a fictional record cover – created to demonstrate creative printing techniques – designed by Hector Pottie, which features a centred symmetrical composition with biaxial symmetry surrounded by white space. Biaxial symmetry means the design is symmetrical in both the vertical and horizontal axes, giving balance in each direction. This balance is complemented by the positioning of the image within the layout, equidistant from each edge.

fictional

Detailed captions
All images are explained through detailed captions.

Chapter overview
Chapter opener pages contain a 'preview' of the chapter ahead, allowing the reader to be familiar with the content.

Key design principles are isolated so that the reader can see how they are applied in practice.

Navigation bar
Chapters are colour coded for easy reference.

Diagrams
Diagrams are used to demonstrate the principles discussed.

Expanded explanations
Analogies are made to explain complex principles.

3.1 The Grid
The grid is a basic design tool used as a guide for the positioning of the various elements used within a design. Over the next few spreads we will dissect the grid, examine its component parts and how they can be used to produce different layouts.

The symmetrical grid
A symmetrical grid presents a layout on the verso page that is a mirror image of that used for the recto page, with equal inner and outer margins. The illustration features proportionally larger outer margins that can accommodate marginalia. The grid also features other main elements such as gutters, head and bottom margins.

The asymmetrical grid
An asymmetrical grid uses the same layout on both the recto and verso pages. The illustration features four narrow text columns as used for the symmetrical grid above, but often asymmetrical grids feature one column that is narrower than the others to introduce a bias towards one side of the page, usually the left. The narrower column may be used as a wide margin for captions, notes, icons or other elements.

The grid analogy
In a rational urge to organise things and we use grids every day. The library shelving pictured here is a well-known example of the order that a grid can bring, as the logical connections between the vertical and horizontal allows us to locate things easily. Grids function in the same way on a page by helping the viewer to navigate around a design in order to extract information.

In practice, the basic grids shown opposite can be transformed into something altogether more elaborate to produce more dynamic results. The grid is the basis of the page and allows for consistency in design, but it is not the final result and should not restrict creativity.

Poster magazine issue 11 (above)
This spread from the eleventh issue of *Poster* magazine by design studio 3 Deep Design uses a grid that bathes the short columns in space, creating a gentle atmosphere that corresponds to the tranquil and dreamy imagery. The grid controls the decorative borders that frame the text and create the margins, which in turn emphasise the space the text sits within.

1.10 The Rise of Modernism
Modernism (1890–1940) as expressed through the cubist, surrealist and Dadaist movements was shaped by the industrialisation and urbanisation of Western society and the need to make sense of these dramatic changes.

Modernists, including the De Stijl, constructivism and Bauhaus movements, departed from the rural and provincial zeitgeist prevalent in the Victorian era, rejecting its values and styles in favour of a cosmopolitanism that embraced the age.

The beginning of modernism, 1890–1910
Functionality and progress, expressed through the maxim of 'form follows function', became the key concerns in the attempt to move beyond the external physical representation of reality, through experimentation, in a struggle to define what should be considered 'modern' as its proponents re-examined every aspect of existence to identify what was preventing progress.

Olympia (above)
French painter Edouard Manet (1832–1883) was one of the first painters to approach modern-life subjects. His work inspired impressionism, with pieces such as Olympia (1863).

ITC Kabel Book (below)
Kabel is a font influenced by stone-carved Roman letters that consists of a few pure and clear geometric forms, as does Johnston Underground font, which has wide, rounded characters (bottom).

geometry & form

1.11 International Style
International or Swiss style was based on the revolutionary principles of the 1920s, such as De Stijl, Bauhaus and Jan Tschichold's *The New Typography*, which became firmly established in the 1950s.

Grids, mathematical principles, minimal decoration and sanserif typography became the norm as design developed to represent universal usefulness, rather than personal expression.

The international style emphasises cleanliness, readability and objectivity characterised by asymmetric layouts, grid use, sanserif typefaces and the use of photography rather than illustrations.

Univers 65
Univers 45

Mies van der Rohe designs (above)
An interior view of the German Pavilion (top), created by architect Mies van der Rohe for the 1929 Barcelona International Exhibition. The glass, travertine and marble pavilion was held to be emblematic of the modern movement. Farnsworth House (bottom), with its vast lawn, is a modernist house in landscape format.

Univers (above)
Univers, a font family of over 50 versions created by Adrian Frutiger, features a numbering system that demonstrates the international style fixation with order. This numbering system, Frutiger's grid, is further explained on page 122.

Examples
Work from contemporary design studios brings the book alive.

Historical references
Key figureheads and events are expanded upon in relevant box-outs.

 Johnston Underground

Modernism's second generation (1930–1945)
Modernism had entered popular culture by the 1930s, with its appearance in everyday life through logos such as that of the London Underground (designed by Edward Johnston), which served the need for a clear, easily recognisable visual symbol. Technological change was a reality affecting everyone's lives, with electricity and cars becoming commonplace. This called for new relationships as communication speed increased, against a backdrop of Marxism and Fascism.

Ludwig Mies van der Rohe
German architect Ludwig Mies van der Rohe (1886–1969) was one of the pioneering masters of modern architecture who sought a new architectural style to represent modern times. Using modern materials, such as industrial steel and plate glass, he defined austere but elegant spaces with a minimal framework of structural order, such as the 197-metre tall Lake Point Tower, built in Chicago, USA in 1968 (left).

Chapter 1 / Historical Context

Since man first began recording information with cuneiform marks in clay tablets there has been the need to organise information. The ancient Egyptians introduced geometry and the ancient Greeks proportion, and the notion of classical style and the presentation of information has developed so that we have little trouble navigating around sophisticated layouts in newspapers, websites or instruction manuals.

This chapter identifies the historical bases of layout as used in graphic design to organise information; many of these are still in use, or are recognisable in the practices we follow today.

No matter how much technology develops, certain eternal principles can still be applied to organise and present information. The fact that we live in the digital age with new media does not mean that classical concepts of balance and harmony are any less important.

Illuminated panel (opposite)

This is an illuminated panel depicting *The Flight into Egypt* and the *Dispute of Jesus in the Temple*. This painting has a clear division of space, with a central column splitting the work area into two. The paintings have top and bottom margins that frame them and also carry information about the images.

Cuneiform tablet (below)

Cuneiform, the earliest known form of writing, was made with a reed stylus pressed into a clay tablet.

This chapter will look at:

1.1 Classical Principles

Geometric principles began to develop in ancient Egypt and evolved into what are now known as classical ideals about proportion, the golden ratio, building techniques and ornamentation that reached their pinnacle in ancient Greece (490–323 BC). Geometry was the foundation for the development of classical principles and perhaps the earliest surviving text is *The Elements of Geometry* (c. 300 BC) by Euclid that contained axioms about plane and three-dimensional geometry known as Euclidean geometry.

The origins of geometry

Geometry, meaning earth measure, arose in ancient Egypt to address the spatial relationships of objects, in order to carry out tasks such as marking out fields in the river Nile flood plain. Rudimentary tools such as the 3-4-5 triangle (see below) helped the Egyptians build their monumental stone architecture.

The Great Pyramid of Cheops (right)

This pyramid is thought to incorporate the golden ratio in its dimensions, as dividing the height (a) by half the base (b) gives a result that is very close to the golden ratio.

The 3-4-5 triangle (right)

The 3-4-5 triangle or rope-stretcher's triangle is a rope knotted into 12 sections that is thought to have been used in ancient Egypt as a means of measuring spaces by physically stretching it until it was taut. The ability to make a right-angled triangle using this rope was a breakthrough in building construction and it remains a cornerstone of design today, providing the basis of the modern idea of design and order.

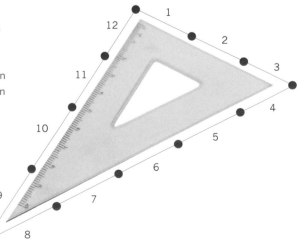

Classicism refers to the predominant characteristics of classical art derived from ancient Greece, such as simplicity, harmony, proportional representation and emotional restraint. Observation of nature and natural proportions helped inform the development of principles such as the golden ratio and became a key influence in Greek art and architecture. Two main styles (orders) were prevalent in Greek architecture – Doric and Ionic – that reflected the Greeks' belief that the styles descended from the Dorian and Ionian Greeks of the Dark Ages. The Doric style is more formal and austere, while the Ionic is more relaxed and decorative. A later development of Ionic is the Corinthian style. The differences between the orders can be seen in the column capitals (as shown at the bottom of this page).

The Parthenon (left)

Pictured is the Parthenon in Athens, Greece, which was built according to the proportions of the golden spiral (below left), which itself uses the proportions established by the golden ratio (8:13). These ratios continue to be used in modern times due to the timeless, classical and harmonious proportions they provide.

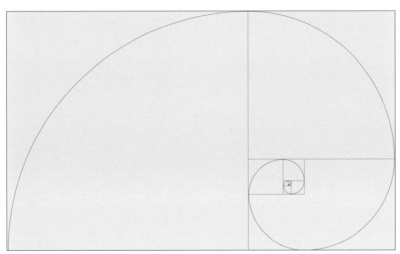

Golden spiral (left)

This is a logarithmic spiral whose growth factor relates to the golden ratio and gets wider by the golden ratio factor for every quarter turn it makes. A Fibonacci spiral approximates this, although it is not a true logarithmic spiral as it gets wider at every quarter turn by a changing factor related to the ratios of consecutive terms in the Fibonacci sequence (see page 48).

The five orders (right)

The five orders or types of columns demonstrate how the design of a single element can alter in proportion and complexity to produce different results, although essentially serving the same function. The same is true of design today, as although columns still serve the same function, they continue to be embellished and styled differently. False columns that look like the classical columns are also used to decorate neo-classical buildings. Left to right: Tuscan, Doric, Ionic, Corinthian and Composite columns.

1.2 Early Manuscripts

The need to communicate and disseminate information and ideas presents quite a challenge, given the limitations of the spoken word in the face of the need to record the accumulation of surplus wealth that could be harnessed for the development of society.

The development of writing allowed historic events and basic accounts to be recorded on manuscripts. The subsequent development of printing allowed wider dissemination of information, which has progressed to the extent that today, in the digital age, communication can be instantaneous and global.

Hieroglyphs (right)
This is a papyrus with ancient Egyptian hieroglyphic characters, which were an early form of writing.

Egyptian hieroglyphs were developed by scribes to record the possessions of the Pharaohs, initially with pictograms representing basic items such as a cow or a boat, for example. As administrative and accounting texts were written on papyrus most employed the Egyptian hieratic script and numeral system, which included individual signs for the numbers one to nine, multiples of ten from ten to 90, the hundreds from 100 to 900, and the thousands from 1,000 to 9,000. Hieratic numerals were ciphered or mapped on to Egyptian letters.

Development (right)
The human ability to communicate continues to develop and evolve, each time enabling a communicator to reach a wider and wider audience.

Oral   Manuscripts   Print   Electronic

Manuscript production was a slow and laborious process to reproduce texts, as it was based on copying an original by hand. The need to distribute more copies saw monks produce 'editions' by copying from a master document, but despite the need to distribute more copies of a text, the production technology did not exist to do this very quickly. As demand for written material continued to grow, it eventually led to the development of new technologies, such as printing (see pages 16–17) and many centuries later, ultimately to the development of electronic media through which a single file can be viewed simultaneously by millions of people.

St Benedict (above)
This is *St Benedict Writing the Rules* by Hermann Nigg (1926), which depicts St Benedict of Nursia (c. 480–543) in the process of writing the precepts for monks that live in community under the authority of an abbot. In the 1500 or so years of its existence it has become a leading guide in Western Christianity to monastic living in community, which is based on peace, prayer and work.

The Book of Kells (left and below)
Pictured is a page and details from the *Book of Kells*, an ornately illustrated manuscript, produced by Celtic monks around AD 800 in the style known as Insular art. It is named after Kells Abbey in County Meath, Ireland, where it was kept for much of the medieval period. The book dates from the late 8th or early 9th century.

1.3 The Development of Printing

Printed publications that we read today are the culmination of centuries of printing technology development. While a modern printing press bears little resemblance to an early wood-block press, it maintains the principle of placing an inked surface in contact with stock under pressure.

Diamond Sutra (right)
This is the *Diamond Sutra* from Dunhuang, China, that dates from AD 868 and is believed to be the oldest printed text in the world. The five-metre scroll is formed of seven strips of paper joined together with an illustration on the first sheet.

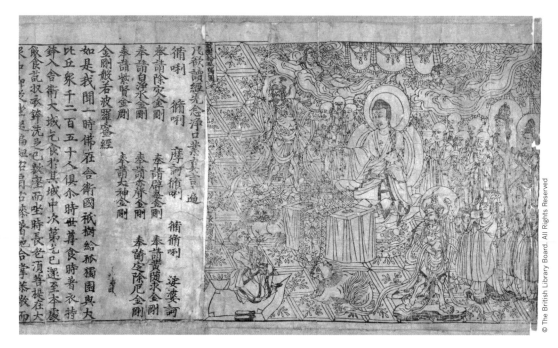

Printing timeline (right)
Since it originated in Tang Dynasty China (AD 618 to AD 906), when inked wooden blocks were first used, printing has seen several milestones. While moveable type appeared in Korea in 1241, Europe did not see wood-block printing until 1423. 19th-century inventions included iron printing presses (1800), offset web press (1863) and Linotype-composing machines (1886).

618–906	Chinese print using carved wooden blocks.
1241	Koreans print books with moveable type.
1300	Chinese use wooden type.
1309	Europeans make paper although already produced in China and Egypt.
1392	Korean foundries produce bronze type.
1423	Europe starts block printing books.
1452	Europe uses metal printing plates.
1501	Italic type used.
1605	The first weekly newspaper is published in Antwerp, Belgium.
1702	Invention of engraving process that prints in different colours.
1800	Invention of iron printing press.
1819	Invention of rotary printing press.
1841	Invention of type-composing machine.
1846	Invention of cylinder press printing 8,000 sheets an hour.
1863	Invention of rotary web-fed letterpress.
1886	Invention of Linotype-composing machine.
1870	Paper mass-manufactured from wood pulp.
1878	Invention of photogravure printing.
1891	Presses print and fold 90,000 four-page papers an hour.
1892	Invention of four-colour rotary press.
1904	Offset lithography common.
1907	Invention of commercial silk-screen printing.
1947	Photo-typesetting commercially practical.

Canons are a general set of design principles that can help guide and assist decision making. Some of these axioms have become firmly established norms, but even though the advice they give is very persuasive and reinforced by centuries of accumulated practice, there is nothing to say that they should not be challenged, adapted or reinterpreted. This page features some canons used to define spaces for text blocks on book pages.

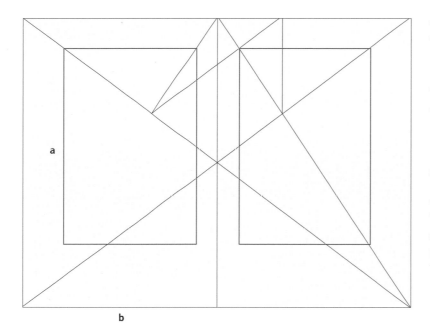

The Van de Graaf canon

The Van de Graaf 'secret' canon is a method used to divide book pages in pleasing proportions. The canon works with any page width:height ratio and allows a designer to position a text block so that page proportions are maintained while creating functional margins of 1/9 and 2/9 of the page size, where the inside margin is one half of the outside margin. This canon, which was adopted by typographer Jan Tschichold, stipulates that the text area and page size share the same proportions, while the height of the text area (a) equals the page width (b).

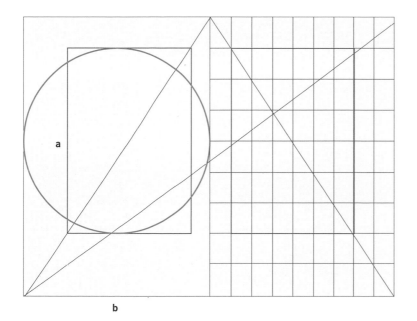

**Tschichold's
'golden canon of page construction'**

Tschichold interpreted the 2:3 proportion that Raúl Rosarivo discussed in his 1947 book *Divina Proporción Tipográfica (Divine typographical proportion)* for his 'golden canon of page construction'. Tschichold's figure combines diagonals and a circle with Rosarivo's division of the page into ninths. Both constructions use the 2:3 page ratio to produce a text block height (a) equal to page width (b) (demonstrated by the circle) with margin proportions of 2:3:4:6.

1.4 The Impact of Moveable Type

The invention of moveable type for printing presses allowed text characters to be reused, which saved on cost and time. The introduction of the printing press allowed for the mass production of books that previously had to be written by hand.

The Gutenberg Bible (right)

The *Gutenberg Bible* was the first printed book in Europe. Its first page (right) features the Epistle of St Jerome from the *Old Testament*. The painted decoration was applied after printing.

Luttrell Psalter (centre)

A 14th-century Luttrell Psalter.

Canterbury Tales (far right)

The Plowman is a portrait of Geoffrey Chaucer as a Canterbury pilgrim from the *Ellesmere Canterbury Tales* manuscript.

Illuminated capitals (right)

Original designs by William Morris.

 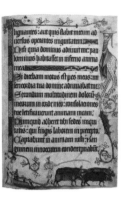 

The development of moveable type saw the first steps towards the industrialisation of the printed word and the first attempts to create structure through layout due to the physical properties of the presses and type blocks used. The use of columns became more common in place of writing across the page, perhaps because it was easier to set type this way. Texts became less ornate, although some were still finished and decorated by hand. Succeeding generations rediscover and incorporate the methods of the past, such as these illuminated characters created by William Morris during the Arts and Crafts Movement; their modern equivalent is the drop cap.

Johannes Gensfleisch zur Laden zum Gutenberg

Johannes Gutenberg (c. 1400–1468) was a German printer who developed the printing press and use of moveable type, which allowed mass book production. His most famous printed work is the *Gutenberg Bible*, which has 42 lines on each page and was printed in 1455.

William Caxton

William Caxton (c. 1422–1492) introduced the printing press to England in 1476 and was the first English printer and bookseller. Pictured (left) is a facsimile of the first page of the only extant copy of *Godefroy of Boloyne* or *Last Siege and Conqueste of Jherusalem* printed in 1481.

The prologue begins: 'Here begynneth the boke Intituled Eracles, and also Godefroy of Boloyne, the whiche speketh of the Conquest of the holy lande of Jherusalem.'

The Renaissance, meaning rebirth, saw the revival of classical concepts of art and beauty in 14th–16th-century Europe and advancements in science, as well as the development of perspective in painting. This classical revision attempted to codify the proportions developed and used by the ancient Greeks.

The Renaissance period was an era pregnant with ideas as a result of the rise of humanism and the study of nature due to people increasingly questioning the world around them. A boost was received when Constantinople fell to the Turks in 1453 and scholars fled westwards, bringing classical Roman and Greek texts and knowledge of classical civilisations with them. This reprise of classical ideas about proportion and style saw a resurgence of concepts, such as the golden ratio, which were applied to layouts as diverse as paintings, gardens and architecture. These rediscovered principles were also applied to book design and the placement of text blocks on a page.

Santa Maria del Fiore (above)

The dome of Santa Maria del Fiore in Florence, Italy, by Filippo Brunelleschi was completed in 1436. Brunelleschi was noted for his work to mathematically understand perspective.

The School of Athens (right)

Florentine Renaissance artist Raphael (1483–1520) depicted classical scenes with the features of his Renaissance contemporaries, such as *The School of Athens*.

1.6 The Arts and Crafts Movement

The Victorian Arts and Crafts Movement developed as a rejection of heavily ornamented interiors with many pieces of furniture, collections of ornamental objects and surfaces covered with fringed cloths, in favour of simplicity, good craftsmanship and design.

Kelmscott Chaucer (right)

Pictured is the *Works of Geoffrey Chaucer* (1896), the masterpiece of the Kelmscott Press, which set a new benchmark in book design. The Press was founded in 1891 and aimed to revive traditional printing methods and craftsmanship in the face of the growing use of lithography. Its publications featured the integration of type and page decoration.

Stairway (above)

A stairway in Glasgow, Scotland, which was created in the Arts and Crafts' style.

19th-century English designer William Morris founded the Kelmscott Press through his desire to revive the skills of hand printing and restore the quality achieved by 15th-century printers. Published in 1896, the *Works of Geoffrey Chaucer* contains 87 wood-engraved illustrations by Edward Burne-Jones and is the masterpiece of the press. The *Kelmscott Chaucer* set a benchmark for book design due to the illustrations and rich decorative borders. 'If we live to finish it, it will be like a pocket cathedral – so full of design, and I think Morris the greatest master of ornament in the world,' wrote Burne-Jones.

Rennie Mackintosh ITC (right)

This font was recut based on designs by Scottish architect, designer and watercolourist Charles Rennie Mackintosh (1868–1928), a leading designer in the Arts and Crafts movement.

ABCDEFGHIJKLMNOPQRSTUVWXYZ
1234567890

Art nouveau, the new art, is a richly ornamented style of decoration, architecture, art and graphic design that developed between 1894 and 1914. It is characterised by undulating lines, sinuous curves and the depiction of leaves, flowers and flowing vines.

Eckmann (right)
This is Eckmann, a font named after designer Otto Eckmann, which has flowing contours that provide a nostalgic feeling.

ABCDEFGHIJKLMNOPQRSTUVWXYZ
abcdefghijklmnopqrstuvwxyz
1234567890

Art nouveau examples (below)
These are various examples of the art nouveau style: a poster by Alphonse Mucha (left); a façade by Antoni Gaudí in Barcelona, Spain (middle); *The Peacock Skirt*, illustration by Aubrey Beardsley for Oscar Wilde's play, *Salomé* (1892) (far right, top); and the cover of Arthur Mackmurdo's 1883 *Wren's City Churches* (far right, bottom).

Called jugendstil in Germany and modernismo in Spain, art nouveau rejected historical references in favour of creating a highly stylised design vocabulary that unified all arts around man and his life. This saw open layouts that gave prominence to decorative images. However, architecture was the main focus for art nouveau, as it naturally encompasses and integrates every art, but the style was also used extensively in posters and jewellery design. Leading protagonists included Gustav Klimt, Henri de Toulouse-Lautrec, Antoni Gaudí and Hector Guimard, the architect and designer of the Paris Metro entrances.

1.8 The Bauhaus

The Bauhaus art and design school (1919–1933) under the direction of renowned architect Walter Gropius aimed to provide a fresh approach to design following the First World War. The style is characterised by a focus on functionality rather than adornment, and the use of geometric forms.

The Bauhaus (above)
Pictured is the exterior of the workshop block of the Bauhaus in Dessau, Germany, which features simple geometric forms and colouring.

Collage M2 439 (right)
German artist Kurt Schwitters (1887–1948) was inspired by Bauhaus typographic designs to create optophonetical type designs whose letterforms visually resemble the sounds connected to them, such as the broad B in *Collage M2 439* (1922).

Bauhaus, which means house for building, focused on producing designs according to first principles rather than by following historic precedent and favoured pure form characterised by economic layouts with geometrical shapes and a low-key palette of white, grey, beige or black. Herbert Bayer paid specific attention to minimalist typographic detailing, for example, such as the removal of capital letters. Far from being merely a fashion, this period provided type and layout that answered the needs of the modern industrialised world with an aesthetic legacy that is still relevant today.

abcdefghijklmnopqrstuvwxyz
1234567890

Bayer Universal (above)
This is P22 Bayer Universal, a unicase font that has no capitals, created by Herbert Bayer, who wanted designs with as few elements as possible.

El Lissitzky
El Lissitzky (1890–1941) was a Russian Jewish artist and proponent of suprematism, which rejected the imitation of natural shapes to focus on the creation of distinct, geometric forms that influenced the subsequent Bauhaus style and 20th-century graphic design. This can be seen in *Beat the Whites with the Red Wedge* (1919) (left), a poster depicting Communism defeating the monarchists during Russia's civil war. Lissitzky designed the cover (right) for issue 8, volume 2, 1924, of *MERZ*, a magazine published between 1923–32 by Kurt Schwitters, which featured radical experiments in poetry and typography.

Art deco is a design style of the early 20th century that celebrated the rise of technology and speed, and borrowed decorative qualities from other movements of the period, such as futurism and cubism. It is characterised by geometric designs, spacious layouts and strong, dynamic lines.

Named after the 1925 Exposition Internationale des Arts Décoratifs et Industriels Modernes, held in Paris, art deco saw forms become streamlined as the principles of aerodynamics became better understood, resulting in elegant architecture, objects and graphic design, with cleaner lines coming to the fore. During this period, designers created layouts that embraced angular and geometric forms, which were accentuated with simple lines representing streamlined and aerodynamic motifs. Layouts also set subject matter in space as part of an uncluttered approach to allow the sleek, angular elements to speak for themselves.

Vogue (left)
Cover of *Vogue* magazine with references to speed and slender, chic human forms characteristic of the art deco age, in a spacious layout.

Vida (bottom left)
This illustration by Santiago Martinez Delgado for Colombia's *Vida* magazine (1938) features a simple, iconic layout.

College Street Store foyer sketch (below)
A pencil drawing of a College Street Store interior featuring open spaces and a sweeping ceiling line.

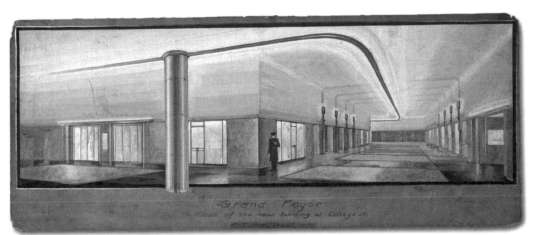

1.10 The Rise of Modernism

Modernism (1890–1940) as expressed through the cubist, surrealist and Dadaist movements was shaped by the industrialisation and urbanisation of Western society and the need to make sense of these dramatic changes.

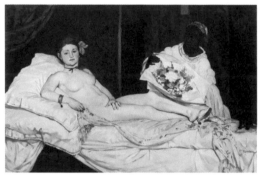

Olympia (above)
French painter Edouard Manet (1832–1883) was one of the first painters to approach modern-life subjects. His work inspired impressionism, with pieces such as *Olympia* (1863).

ITC Kabel Book (below)
Kabel is a font influenced by stone-carved Roman letters that consists of a few pure and clear geometric forms, as does Johnston Underground font, which has wide, rounded characters (bottom).

Modernists, including the De Stijl, constructivism and Bauhaus movements, departed from the rural and provincial zeitgeist prevalent in the Victorian era, rejecting its values and styles in favour of a cosmopolitanism that embraced the age.

The beginning of modernism, 1890–1910
Functionality and progress, expressed through the maxim of 'form follows function', became the key concerns in the attempt to move beyond the external physical representation of reality, through experimentation, in a struggle to define what should be considered 'modern' as its proponents re-examined every aspect of existence to identify what was preventing progress.

geometry & form

Johnston Underground

Modernism's second generation (1930–1945)
Modernism had entered popular culture by the 1930s, with its appearance in everyday life through logos such as that of the London Underground (designed by Edward Johnston), which served the need for a clear, easily recognisable visual symbol. Technological change was a reality affecting everyone's lives, with electricity and cars becoming commonplace. This called for new relationships as communication speed increased, against a backdrop of Marxism and Fascism.

International or Swiss style was based on the revolutionary principles of the 1920s, such as De Stijl, Bauhaus and Jan Tschichold's *The New Typography*, which became firmly established in the 1950s.

Grids, mathematical principles, minimal decoration and sanserif typography became the norm as design developed to represent universal usefulness, rather than personal expression.

The international style emphasises cleanliness, readability and objectivity characterised by asymmetric layouts, grid use, sanserif typefaces and the use of photography rather than illustrations.

Univers 65
Univers 45

Mies van der Rohe designs (above)
An interior view of the German Pavilion (top), created by architect Mies van der Rohe for the 1929 Barcelona International Exhibition. The glass, travertine and marble pavilion was held to be emblematic of the modern movement. Farnsworth House (bottom), with its vast lawn, is a modernist house in landscape format.

Univers (above)
Univers, a font family of over 50 versions created by Adrian Frutiger, features a numbering system that demonstrates the international style fixation with order. This numbering system, Frutiger's grid, is further explained on page 122.

Ludwig Mies van der Rohe
German architect Ludwig Mies van der Rohe (1886–1969) was one of the pioneering masters of modern architecture who sought a new architectural style to represent modern times. Using modern materials, such as industrial steel and plate glass, he defined austere but elegant spaces with a minimal framework of structural order, such as the 197-metre tall Lake Point Tower, built in Chicago, USA in 1968 (left).

1.12 Graphic Design Today

Graphic design as a discipline emerged in the 1950s from what was known as commercial art, with much of the terminology it uses borrowed from other disciplines such as art, literature, photography and psychology.

Design Quarterly (above left)

This is the Paul Rand Miscellany cover for *Design Quarterly* that features truncated type. Although only parts of the letters are visible we can still read what it says.

Design today (right and above right)

Graphic design was the tool used to build brands and educate people to consume, but the appropriation of the US flag (above) by anti-consumerist magazine *Adbusters* highlights the changing role of the maturing graphic design industry as it seeks to question and reduce consumption. This spread from a book by Sophie Calle created by Frost Design (right) is an example of the power of the graphic image.

Constructivism

This is a modern art movement that originated in Moscow around 1920, characterised by the use of industrial materials, such as glass, sheet metal and plastic to create non-representational, abstract, often geometric objects, as it fully embraced modernity. Leading constructivist practitioners include Wassily Kandinsky, Alexander Rodchenko and El Lissitzky. Pictured is *The Constructor* (1925), a self-portrait photomontage of Lissitzky.

Avant-garde

Works that pushed the limits of what was considered acceptable, often with revolutionary, cultural, or political connotations, such as Marcel Duchamp's *LHOOQ*, a copy of da Vinci's *Mona Lisa* embellished with graffiti.

Suprematism

Suprematism is an art movement formed in Russia in 1913 by Kasimir Malevich, which focused on the fundamental geometric forms of squares and circles. Pictured are *Black Circle* and *Black Square* (both 1913) by Kasimir Malevich, which are displayed in the State Russian Museum in St Petersburg.

Dadaism

Dada was an art movement (1916–1920) of European writers and artists led by French poet Tristan Tzara, which fomented anarchic revolt and the role of chance in the creative process. Outraged by the carnage of the First World War, Dadaists aimed to shock people through their irreverence for established norms, such as *Fountain* by Marcel Duchamp (1917), which is an inverted urinal (above left). Dadaist and surrealist photographer Man Ray (1934) by Carl Van Vechten (above right).

Futurism

Futurism was a Russian and Italian movement across the range of creative disciplines that exhibited a passionate loathing of ideas from the past, such as political and artistic traditions. With the car and aircraft becoming increasingly popular, speed and technology and the technological triumph of man over nature were the tenets, with those sticking to the old ways labelled 'pastists'. Pictured (above left) is *Riot in the Galleria* (1910) by Italian futurist painter Umberto Boccioni, which focuses on the portrayal of movement. This satirical agitprop poster (above right) is by Vladimir Mayakovsky.

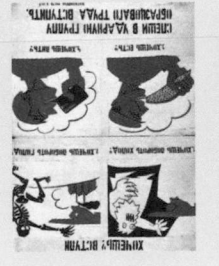

Fuse (above)

This is a poster from issue 11 of typographical magazine *Fuse*, created by Fuel design studio, which features 'anti-type', with letters that appear to have been produced with strips of tape.

* A reaction to modernism, postmodernism returned to earlier ideas of adornment and decoration, celebrating expression and personal intuition in favour of formula and structure. A famous example of this was a 1994 interview with singer Brian Ferry published in *Ray Gun* magazine. David Carson, its radical art director, decided to print the interview entirely in a symbol font that made the double-page spread illegible.

1.13 Postmodernism

A creative movement (1960–present) that developed following the Second World War and questioned the very notion that there is a reliable reality. It deconstructed authority and the established order by engaging in fragmentation, incoherence and the plain ridiculous.

1.14 Deconstruction

Deconstruction refers to a postmodernist critical approach initially expounded by Jacques Derrida, which seeks to undermine the frame of reference and assumptions behind a pattern of thought to explore the way that meaning is constructed.

Influenced by Friedrich Nietzsche, Derrida argued that the existence of deconstruction implied that there was no intrinsic essence to a text, merely the contrast of difference. This includes the discovery and understanding of underlying, unspoken and implicit assumptions, ideas and frameworks that form the basis for thought and belief. French philosopher Michel Foucault helped popularise the concept through his deconstruction of history and subjectivity as he criticised traditional historical analysis.

Zembla (right)

This is *Zembla* magazine, created by design studio Frost Design, in which normally passive areas of the spread become self-conscious focal points. While there is a strong sense of the grid and layout, it is also intentionally ignored to create movement and pace across the spread, for example, by making the gutter active in the tension of the design.

Michel Foucault

French philosopher Michel Foucault (1926–1984) produced critical studies of various social institutions and was known for his work on sexuality, the relation between power and knowledge, and ideas about the history of Western thought.

Jacques Derrida

Algerian-born French philosopher Jacques Derrida (1930–2004) introduced deconstruction in a 1966 paper as an attempt to open a text to several meanings and interpretations, based on culturally and historically defined binary oppositions.

Friedrich Nietzsche (right)

Prussian-born philosopher Friedrich Nietzsche (1844–1900) identified binary oppositions as he examined the difference between good and bad, and good and evil, for example. He had a profound influence on existentialism, postmodernism, psychoanalysis, libertarianism and most subsequent thought movements.

Manifestation in graphic design layout refers to the use of practices or methods that are atypical and often experimental. A grid to assist page element positioning is normally invisible in the printed job, but in some instances it can be evident and clearly visible. In the same vein, schools, such as Cranbrook Academy, for instance, borrow principles taught in a discipline, such as philosophy, and use them as a tool for unpicking, or deconstructing another, such as graphic design.

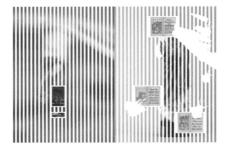 

**Experimentation
(above and left)**
Andy Altmann of Why Not Associates design studio challenges the notion of the grid. In this case, the grid becomes a road to freedom, rather than a restriction to the placement of elements.

Richard Eckersley

This is Avital Ronell's *Telephone Book: Technology, Schizophrenia, Electric Speech* (1989) created by award-winning book designer Richard Eckersley. Each page questions conventional page layout through the use of graphic marks, the deliberate creation of rivers, irregular spacing and text framing as part of a radical approach towards visual experimentation in layout and typographic treatment of the texts.

Pluralism

Pluralism implies embracing multiple narratives, rather than one, being expansive and all encompassing rather than maintaining a narrow, restrictive viewpoint, which is where we find contemporary graphic design.

Chapter 2 / Principles

All design is undertaken with reference to a certain set of principles, either by consciously choosing to follow or by deliberately ignoring or subverting them. The collective body of principles represents different approaches to design and layout construction.

The principles in this section have been used through the ages to produce designs that are pleasing to the eye and that organise information clearly and efficiently, two of the challenges facing every graphic designer. These principles affect decisions made at the heart of the design process, as they provide the basis of how space is divided. Many principles originate from the need to solve specific problems, such as the Renard numbers used in this image (opposite).

Renard series of numbers (opposite)
Pictured is a proposal sketch for a wall-hanging design created by Claire Gordon Interiors that uses the Renard series of preferred numbers. The Renard series offers a controlled approach to space division, which produces a balanced design while allowing a degree of dynamic randomness as the proportions of the stripes are largely chosen by 'eye'. Variations on this mathematical series can be adopted using different square roots, as shown on page 052.

This chapter will look at:

2.1 The Process of Design

Before examining design principles in detail it is worth taking a look at the design process in isolation. A design serves to communicate a specific piece of information or perform a specific function, and the design process will inform the result.

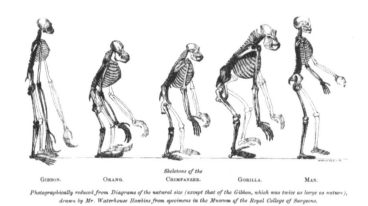

GIBBON.   ORANG.   *Skeletons of the* CHIMPANZEE.   GORILLA.   MAN.

Photographically reduced from Diagrams of the natural size (except that of the Gibbon, which was twice as large as nature), drawn by Mr. Waterhouse Hawkins from specimens in the Museum of the Royal College of Surgeons.

Approaches to design (right)
This illustration shows morphological similarities in the *Hominidæ* family to which humans (*Homo sapiens*) belong, which shows evidence of common descent. The evolution of the *Hominidæ* family provides a visual analogy of how different approaches to design can produce different, yet equally valid solutions.

What is a design?
A design serves as a medium for recording, presenting, ordering and communicating information about a specific intention or function. For example, an architect's blueprints record, present and order information about a building design. The intention to communicate detailed and precise information is the start of the design process and influences the choices made throughout its duration, such as how the information is presented, in what format and in what level of detail.

The intention of a design
Nowadays it is common for a company to have a mission statement that expresses its core values and aims, but there is nothing new about this. The most famous manifesto is probably the Declaration of Independence, written by Thomas Jefferson in 1776, which outlined the intention of the former British colonies to seek independence and become the USA. It begins 'When, in the course of human events, it becomes necessary for one people to dissolve the political bonds which have connected them with another....'

Design intentions (above)
A detail from the Declaration of Independence (top), an example of a statement of intent, and the cover of the Dada manifesto (bottom).

Several important artistic and social movements have also presented manifestos that influenced the work they produced. Tristan Tzara et al. wrote the Dada manifesto in 1918, which begins 'DADA!!!! gathered together to put forward a new art from which they expect the realization of new ideas. So what is DADAISM, then? The word DADA symbolizes the most primitive relationship with the surrounding reality; with Dadaism, a new reality comes into its own.' In Germany, the overriding viewpoint of the Bauhaus school (1919–1933) was that 'The ultimate aim of all creative activity is a building!' as it sought a fusion of design-based arts.

The intention of a design will often be as simple (or complicated) as a design brief that outlines the objective and purpose of a project. However, as these examples illustrate, there is often a higher overriding leitmotif, or symbolic idea, that directs the development of the design and that guides every project created by a design studio.

Ultimately, all designers work towards specific goals and several methodologies have been developed for use in design, whether the ultimate aim is to produce a magazine spread or a chair. There is no prescriptive method to layout design and it is often the variance that comes from using different methods that results in innovative design. 'Breaking the mould' essentially means using a different approach or methodology to arrive at a different design solution, whether the design is for packaging, book covers, Web pages, furniture or interior spaces.

Featured below are various methodologies that can be used as a starting framework for producing a design.

User-centred design

The user-centred design (UCD) approach places the needs, desires and limitations of the user at the centre of every stage of the design process. This multi-stage problem-solving process requires designers to foresee how users are likely to use the resulting product and test the validity of these assumptions in real-world tests with actual users. Real-world testing enables designers to understand what a user experiences the first time they use the design or product and what their learning curve may be.

Use-centred design

The use-centred design approach focuses on the goals and tasks associated with the use of a design, rather than focusing on the needs, desires and limitations of the user in the user-centred approach.

Axiomatic design

The axiomatic design approach uses axioms – elements given without proof – to govern the decision-making process as it seeks to transform user needs into functional requirements and design parameters. The approach reduces client needs into functional requirements, which are used to create design parameters.

KISS

The KISS (keep it simple, stupid) principle highlights the fact that simplicity is a desirable objective in producing effective designs. For example, during the Cold War, while NASA spent a vast amount of money to develop a pen that astronauts could use in zero gravity, Russian cosmonauts simply used a pencil.

Bottom up

A bottom-up design approach uses the characteristics of the individual elements as the basis for decision making. For example, with text and photos for an article in hand, a magazine layout is created taking into account the characteristics of these elements, so as to maximise the impact of the photography, present detailed information and so on. Many magazines use this approach to produce creative spreads in harmony with the visual and textual content.

Python philosophy

Derived from computer programming, the main points of the Python approach were presented by developer Tim Peters in *The Zen of Python*. Key points include: beautiful is better than ugly, explicit is better than implicit, simple is better than complex, complex is better than complicated, sparse is better than dense, readability counts, special cases are not special enough to break the rules, practicality beats purity, errors should never pass silently, and refuse the temptation to guess.

TIMTOWTDI

There is more than one way to do it (TIMTOWTDI pronounced Tim Toady) follows the belief that a problem may have several different, but equally valid solutions.

Lateral thinking

Lateral thinking is a design approach that looks to change concepts and perceptions in order to arrive at different solutions by looking for what is not immediately obvious, and solutions that may not be obtainable using traditional step-by-step logic.

Occam or Ockham's razor

14th-century English logician and Franciscan Friar, William of Ockham, is attributed with this principle that forms the basis of methodological reductionism. The principle states that elements that are not really needed should be pared back to produce something simpler. This reduces the risk of introducing inconsistencies, ambiguities and redundancies. This is a minimalist approach.

Top down

A top-down design approach sees a designer create the basic design before the elements that will be placed within it are available. For example, a designer may create templates into which text and photos can be dropped as and when needed. Most newspapers and many websites use the top-down approach as it gives total control over presentation and positioning.

Approaches to Design

An approach to design is the general philosophy or conceptual outline that guides and influences choices made by the designer during the design process. Some approaches are very functional and guided by the overall goal of the design project, such as making a very user-friendly website with intuitive navigation through different levels of complex information, or creating a magazine spread to maximise the impact of the photography. A design approach may also reflect the trademark style of a particular designer or a particular cultural zeitgeist, such as the pastel colour palette that was popular in the 1980s.

The design process has various different stages depending upon its complexity and the budget available. Typically, it can be broken down into pre-production, design production and post-production. Pre-production includes the design brief and statement of the design goals; for example, the creation of a mailer for a compact disc that makes more of a statement than merely putting it in a protective envelope.

A design studio may research the different solutions already available and what it has used in the past in addition to finding out more about the product and its target market. This information feeds into the specification of the solution and the creation of preliminary designs and mock-ups. During the production phase, a design studio continues the development of the chosen solution and refines it until it meets the design brief and it is accepted by the client. For example, the CD mailer design is developed so that it serves both the packaging (protecting the CD) and communication functions. The layout/design is developed to incorporate the physical format requirements of the mailer, such as how it will be folded, the visual impact the client is seeking, and practical considerations, such as space for adding addresses to the mailers. Post-production sees the implementation of the design solution and an evaluation of its success and effectiveness in meeting the client's goals.

Dieter Rams (right)
This is a statement by Dieter Rams, a product designer associated with electrical appliance manufacturer Braun, expounding the key to good design.

'To me good design means as little design as possible.
Simple is better than complicated.
Quiet is better than loud.
Unobtrusive is better than exciting.
Small is better than large.
Light is better than heavy.
Plain is better than coloured.
Harmony is better than divergency.
Being well balanced is better than being exalted.
Continuity is better than change.
Sparse is better than profuse.
Neutral is better than aggressive.
The obvious is better than that which must be sought.
Few elements are better than many.
A system is better than single elements.'

Design preferences change as design adapts to changes in tastes and fashions (zeitgeist – see page 056). Technology also influences the perpetually shifting sands of design by increasing the creative options available. For example, mobile telephones now contain cameras and Web browsers, and printing technology continues to evolve.

Technology

A key element in changing design patterns is the continual development of the technology available to the design and printing industries. For example, the evolution from one-colour to four-colour to six-colour printing has seen colour become ubiquitous, while paper-coating technology enables glossy magazines to obtain photographic reproduction quality that is similar to a photographic print.

Style

Dress hemlines go up, down and up again as style and the zeitgeist changes with increasing velocity. Graphic design changes over time too, as the magazine covers above clearly show. For example, even relatively conservative publications now feature covers of women dressed in a way that in previous times would have been considered unacceptable or even pornographic.

Fads and fashions

Fads and fashions are constantly evolving in the creative arts as people look for the fresh and new, whether in music, fashion, art, architecture or magazine design. Design inspiration often comes from revisiting and reusing fads and fashions from previous decades, particularly given the cycles of action and reaction (below).

Rubbish theory

Michael Thompson's rubbish theory states that items increase and decrease in value over time. Design ideas also rise and fall over time and return when there is a renaissance or rediscovery of methods that were previously used. Typographers create typefaces based on those they have discovered in ancient books, for example, while cut-up, photocopied punk fanzines inspire modern designs targeted at teenagers.

Magazines (above left)
These magazine covers convey a sense of how design tastes and attitudes change over time. These publications were formerly called periodicals because they were published at regular intervals – *GQ* means Gentlemen's Quarterly – but nowadays we call them magazines. This is a paradigm shift from something solid and dependable to something ephemeral, disposable and less important, even though both create, reflect and are influenced by contemporary culture. Layout and typography are essential parts of this symbiotic cultural process.

The Fashion Cycle	
Indecent	10 years before its time
Shameless	5 years before its time
Outré	1 year before its time
Smart	–
Dowdy	1 year after its time
Hideous	10 years after its time
Ridiculous	20 years after its time
Amusing	30 years after its time
Quaint	40 years after its time
Charming	70 years after its time
Romantic	100 years after its time
Beautiful	150 years after its time

Rubbish Theory

Transient (decreasing value)
New furniture is wonderful to have, but loses its allure and value after it has seen several years' use and may even become obsolete.

Rubbish (no value)
A misshapen 15-year-old sofa that is full of dust and dirt has very little value if any.

Durability (increasing value)
Furniture becomes collectable because it is representative of a particular time, such as Bakelite telephones from the 1930s. Older still, it becomes antique.

The fashion cycle (far left)
This was developed by James Laver in *Taste and Fashion* in 1945 and shows how people's reaction to a fashion change and mellow over time. This cycle is now known as Laver's Law.

Rubbish theory (left)
Michael Thompson's rubbish theory presents the idea that something has a value that decreases and eventually increases.

2.2 Relative and Absolute Measurements

Measurement is an integral part of layout and design, from the spatial dimensions of the page, to how the different text and picture elements are spaced. An understanding of various measurement concepts helps underpin and deepen knowledge about layout design.

Absolute measurement

Absolute measurements are based on fixed values. A millimetre is a precisely defined increment of a centimetre, for example. In typography, points and picas are basic units of measurement that have fixed and absolute values. All absolute measurements are expressed in finite terms that cannot be altered. For simplicity, most of these are rational numbers, that is whole numbers. For example, 11mm is rational while 1.1cm is irrational.

Absolute measurements (right)

Pictured is a detail of a tape measure that is used to make absolute (rational) measurements. The divisions have to be fine enough to function as a rational set of numbers. For measurements finer than a centimetre, millimetres are used.

Measurements in design

In practice, a designer will use a mix of different absolute measurements in a layout for different purposes. For example, it is common for the dimensions of a print document to be set up in millimetres that relate to standard paper sizes such as A4 (210mm x 297mm). Type and leading, however, are typically set in points, such as 12pt type on 14pt leading.

Measurement systems (right)

These four bars all have the same absolute length, but in graphic design this can be expressed in several different, but equally valid ways including inches, millimetres, points and picas.

5.117" (5.117 inches)

130 millimetres (130mm)

368.41pt (368.41 points)

30p8.41 (30 picas and 8.41 points)

Many values in typography, such as character spacing, fractions and dashes are directly linked to typesize, which means they are defined by a series of relative measurements rather than absolute measurements. The advantage of this is that elements defined this way are always directly linked to the typesize in which they are set. As the typesize changes so does the relative size of these elements. The basic measurement unit for typographic characters such as these is the em, a measurement that relates to the width of the widest character block, which is often the majuscule 'M', which is itself directly related to the typesize. For example, type set at 12pt has a 12pt em.

Ems and ens
An em is a relative unit of measurement derived from the width of the square body of the metal cast majuscule 'M' and equals the size of a given type. For example, type set at 24pt has a 24pt em. An en is equal to half of one em.

The golden section
The proportions of the golden section appear in many disciplines including art, design and architecture. However, its use in modern society has diminished as the geometric principles on which it is based have taken a back seat to the use of linear measurements. Desktop publishing packages that graphic designers work with use measurements rather than proportions, for example. One of the original uses of the golden section or golden ratio was to define paper sizes.

Width-to-height ratios
Dynamic rectangles or root rectangles are a series of rectangles that extend from the diagonal of a rectangle. Each rectangle drawn from this diagonal has the same width-to-height ratio as the others. Use of these rectangles emphasises the geometrical proportions of the rectangle rather than their actual measurements. Rectangles constructed in this manner can be used in layouts to define text boxes, for example, as described further on page 064.

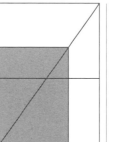

8

The Pacific Railway (right)

The Pacific Railway (1916), by Gaetano Previati, has a canvas size with the 8:13 proportion of the golden section.

2, 3, 4 and 5 dynamic rectangles (far right)
A root 2 rectangle has the same width-to-height ratio as two rectangles of the same size laid side by side, a root 3 rectangle uses three rectangles and so on. These produce rectangles with the following proportions: Root 2 1:1.414, Root 3 1:1.732, Root 4 1:2, Root 5 1:2.236.

13

Root 2 *1 x 1.414*

Root 3 *1 x 1.732*

Root 4 *1 x 2*

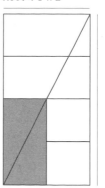

Root 5 *1 x 2.236*

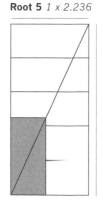

2.2_Relative and Absolute Measurements

2.3 Proportion

Proportion is the visual or structural relationship between part of an item to the whole, such as the relationship between the size of the text boxes to the overall page, for example. Proportion is a useful tool for achieving a balanced layout by helping to define the size relationship that governs the different design elements, such as their relative size and spacing.

The approximate ratio 8:13 was thought by the ancients to represent infallibly beautiful proportions. Dividing a line by this ratio means that the relationship between the greater part of the line and the smaller part is the same as that of the greater part to the whole, and this is the golden section represented by the Greek letter phi.

Objects and designs based on these proportions are particularly pleasing to the eye. In the field of graphic arts, the golden section forms the basis of paper sizes due to the harmonious proportions it provides, and its principles can be used as a means to achieving balanced designs. The golden section is not to be confused with the golden mean, the middle point between two extremes, or with golden numbers, an indicator of years in astronomy and calendar studies.

The golden section in nature
The 8:13 ratio of the golden section is present in the natural world and can be found in the natural growth patterns of snail shells, sunflower seeds, honeycombs and in dolphins where the eye, fins and tail fall at golden sections of the length of its body.

In nature (right)
These natural objects all show the 8:13 golden section ratio in their growth patterns or formation.

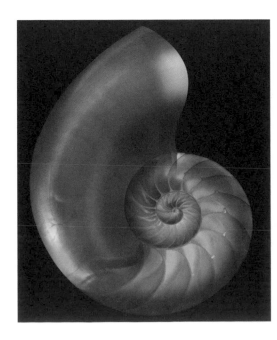

Golden sections can be drawn in one of two ways that also reflect the difference between a measurement-based solution and a geometric solution. While both produce the same result, they differ in the intention behind the selection of each method and their practical application, which ultimately reflects the work practice and medium used by a designer. For example, are exact measurements or proportions more important?

Constructing a golden section using geometry

Pictured is the sequence for drawing a golden section with a compass and set square. This method produces the golden section proportions and has less emphasis on the exact measurements. Begin with a square (A) and dissect it (B). Then form an isosceles triangle (C) by drawing lines from the bottom corners to the top of the bisecting line. Next, extend an arc from the apex of the triangle to the baseline (D) and draw a line perpendicular to the baseline from the point at which the arc intersects it. Complete the rectangle to form the golden section (E).

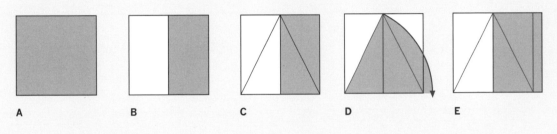

A   B   C   D   E

Geometry (above)
Pictured above is a detail from a medieval painting depicting the teaching of geometry. The illustrations (left) show how a golden section can be drawn using a compass and set square.

Constructing a golden section using mathematics

A golden section can also be constructed using a simple mathematical calculation. Draw a line (A) and divide it in the ratio of 8:13 (B). Each part of the line can be used as the long side from which to draw a golden rectangle using the golden ratio 1:1.618 (C). The long side equates to the 1.618 part of the ratio. To find the length of the short side, divide the long side length by 1.618 and multiply by 1.

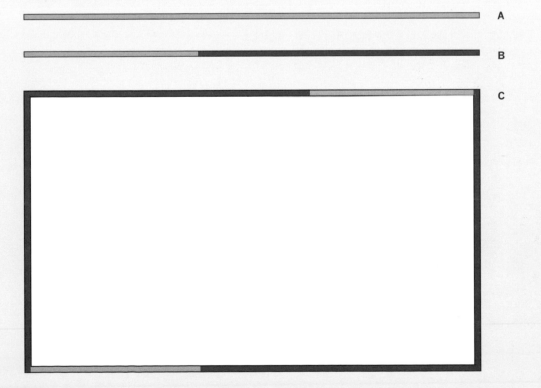

A

B

C

The golden rectangle (left)
The golden rectangle constructed using a full line for the long edge, and a ratio of 1.618 for the short edge. The application of this shape appears in print (design), art and architecture.

Application

The golden section can be seen in use everyday as it is the basis of standard paper sizes. Its presence can also be seen in architecture, canvas sizes and many other applications. In layout, in addition to page size, the golden section can be used to create a basic grid that divides a page and provides space for the different elements that need to be included. The illustration below shows how a page divided using the principles of the golden section produces an area for a text block that has varying amounts of margin space around it, which results in a page or spread with a balanced feel.

Proportion (right)
This illustration represents a drawing by German typographer Jan Tschichold (1902–1974) for an octavo-format page that has the proportions of the golden ratio; in this case the sides are in the ratio 34:21. The text area and margin proportions are determined by the starting page proportions.

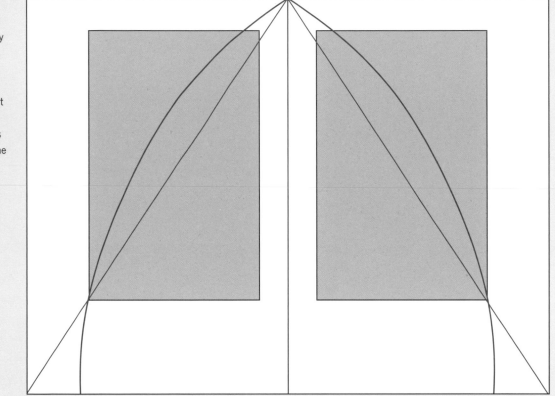

Harmonious relationships

The reason for the success of page layouts, such as that pictured above, is the harmonious spatial relationship that the use of the golden ratio produces. Essentially this is because the division of the page is based on its own proportions. The ancient Greeks used this ratio in the design of many of their buildings.

Pheidias
This is *Pheidias and the Frieze of the Parthenon* by Dutch-born English painter Sir Lawrence Alma-Tadema (1836–1912). Phidias or Pheidias (c. 490–430 BC) was an Athenian sculptor and perhaps more importantly, he was the artistic director of the Parthenon in Athens during its construction. The temple features the golden ratio in several of its elements and through the paintings Pheidias provided for it, he established the visual conceptions of the gods Zeus and Athena.

The golden ratio has been used by many painters in the composition of their works as a means for locating key subject matter on focal points and of spacing the different elements of the composition. The golden ratio can be applied to any spatial relationship in the graphic arts, including design, such as object spacing, text and picture box location, pattern form and so on. It is demonstrated here with paintings.

Bathers at Asnières (left)

Pictured is *Bathers at Asnières* painted by Georges Seurat in 1884. The image is illustrated with the space divided using the golden ratio. It is evidently clear that the location of key and secondary focal points in the composition corresponds to the junction of the golden ratios to create harmonious distances between them.

The Golden Stairs (left)

Pictured left is *The Golden Stairs* by Edward Burne-Jones who also used the golden ratio as a guide for the composition. The starting position of the stairs on the left side was chosen by the 8:13 ratio, as was their mid point on the right side of the canvas, in addition to several other elements in the work.

Phi

Phi, the first letter in the name of Athenian sculptor Phidias, is used to symbolise the golden ratio, as he frequently used it in his work. The lowercase form (φ) represents the golden ratio, while the uppercase form (Φ) represents the reciprocal of the golden ratio, 1/Φ. For example, the length of gown and the position of the knee in the *The Golden Stairs* (above) is phi.

Rule of Thirds

The rule of thirds is a method that is typically used by photographers to form interesting compositions, although it can be applied equally to composition in any of the graphic arts and even disciplines such as textile and furniture design. The rule of thirds can be used to create focal points that can guide where elements of interest are positioned.

The rule of thirds (left)
This diagram shows how the rule of thirds can be used to create hot spots in a layout or design. As you can see, the points where these hot spots fall do not correspond to an exact mathematical division of the area. These are active hot spots because studies have shown that the eye lingers on these points as they scan an image. Designers use this knowledge to guide the positioning of elements to help viewers access key information. A practical application of this is the positioning of navigation bars to the top and left on most websites, and why logos are often placed top left.

Triumph of Galatea (left)
Triumph of Galatea is a fresco painted by Raphael (1512) for the Villa Farnesina in Rome. Galatea, the central figure, is framed by the magenta lines we have used to divide the image. Above her, three cherubs are placed symmetrically with their arrowheads falling above the upper hot spots.

The Luncheon of the Boating Party (above)
The Luncheon of the Boating Party by Pierre-Auguste Renoir (1881) shows how the interaction of the characters is aided by the spatial tension and relationship that is provided by positioning them proportionally according to the rule of thirds.

The visual centre does not refer to the mathematical centre of an image or design, but to a point that is slightly higher and to the right of this, as illustrated below. The visual centre provides an active focal point in a work that can be exploited to provide a hot spot where a viewer's gaze will linger.

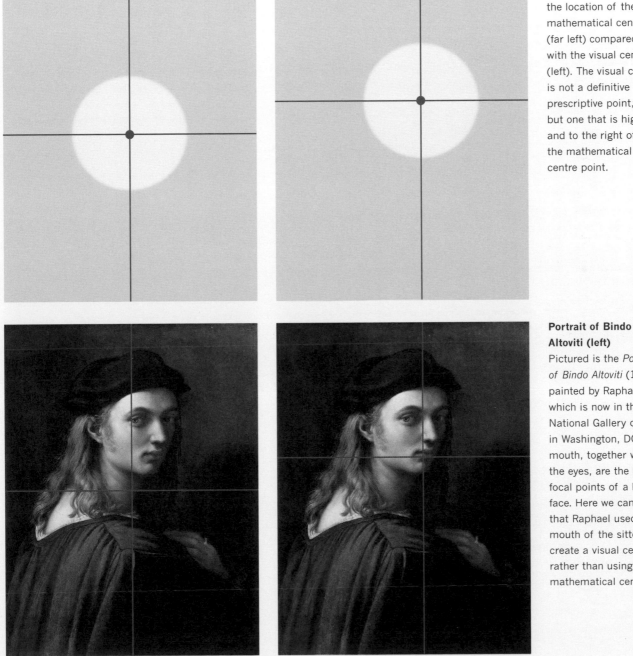

Centres (left)
These diagrams show the location of the mathematical centre (far left) compared with the visual centre (left). The visual centre is not a definitive or prescriptive point, but one that is higher and to the right of the mathematical centre point.

Portrait of Bindo Altoviti (left)
Pictured is the *Portrait of Bindo Altoviti* (1514), painted by Raphael, which is now in the National Gallery of Art in Washington, DC. The mouth, together with the eyes, are the key focal points of a human face. Here we can see that Raphael used the mouth of the sitter to create a visual centre, rather than using the mathematical centre.

Human Proportions

People are very curious about themselves, other people and humanity in general. This curiosity about the human form has also been expressed in design, and throughout history, interest in the proportions of the human body has seen different people try to use it for practical applications.

The ancient Egyptians developed specific measurements based on the human form, such as the cubit, a measure of the length from a Pharaoh's elbow to the farthest fingertip of his extended hand. In this way, the body's proportions have been used in art and architecture to guide the selection of dimensions.

Page layout and the relationship between elements and characters on a page, and the spaces between them, bear similarities to proportions of the body and it is possible that some proportions that have been in common usage originated from observation of the human form. This is unsurprising given that a grid used in layout is the 'bone structure' of a design, working like a skeleton to house the different design elements.

Vitruvian Man

Leonardo da Vinci's *Vitruvian Man* is a world-renowned drawing from c. 1492 that is displayed in the Gallerie dell' Accademia in Venice, Italy. The drawing also contains notes made by Leonardo in his mirror writing (writing in reverse as a primitive form of cipher) on his observations of the human form. The drawing depicts a nude male in two superimposed positions with arms and legs apart, inscribed in a circle and square. The document is sometimes called the *Canon of Proportions* or *Proportions of Man*.

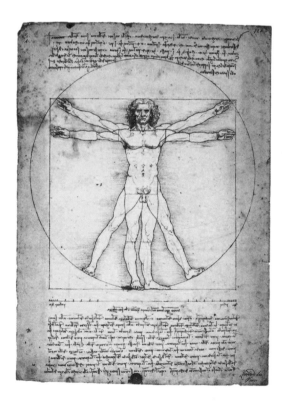

Vitruvian Man (above)

Pictured is Leonardo's *Vitruvian Man*, a sketch about the proportions of the human body.

Leonardo made the *Vitruvian Man* **diagram as part of a study of human proportions based on the observations made by Roman architect Vitruvius. Vitruvius observed that:**

A palm = the width of four fingers

A foot = the width of four palms

A cubit = the width of six palms

A man's height = four cubits (24 palms)

A pace = four cubits

The length of a man's outspread arms = his height

The distance from the hairline to the bottom of the chin = one-tenth of a man's height

The distance from the top of the head to the bottom of the chin = one-eighth of a man's height

The maximum width of the shoulders = a quarter of a man's height

The distance from the elbow to the tip of the hand = one-fifth of a man's height

The distance from the elbow to the armpit = one-eighth of a man's height

The length of the hand = one-tenth of a man's height

The distance from the bottom of the chin to the nose = one-third of the length of the head

The distance from the hairline to the eyebrows = one-third of the length of the face

The length of the ear = one-third of the length of the face

Anthropometry means measurement of humans and refers to the measurement of living human individuals in order to understand physical variation. Anthropometry is increasingly used in industrial design, ergonomics and architecture to develop products that fit better to the human form, using statistical data about the body dimensions of the population to optimise products and building spaces. Characterising the dimensions of the human body is a moving target however, as changes in lifestyle, nutrition and ethnic composition create changes in body dimensions, such as the increasing number of obese people in the West. While far from prescriptive, anthropometric data may be considered to help create designs that more accurately reflect human proportions.

The nose, as it cannot be disguised, is extremely important in identification. The types above, taking them from the left, show a low, narrow nose, a hooked nose, a straight nose, a snub nose, and a high, wide nose.

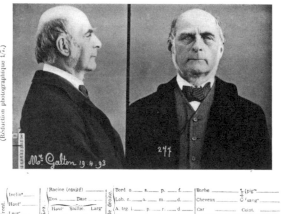

Anthropometry (left)
Human curiosity has led many people to observe and measure people to find clues about our proportions and to answer why we are all different sizes. Pictured (left) is an illustration from *The Speaking Portrait*, from a 1901 issue of *Pearson's Magazine*, demonstrating the principles of anthropometry deduced by Alphonse Bertillon.

The chart (far left) from Bertillon's *Identification anthropométrique* (1893) shows how to take measurements for his identification system. These photos (left) of Francis Galton were taken during a visit to Bertillon's laboratory in 1893. These images are all from Karl Pearson's *The Life, Letters, and Labours of Francis Galton, vol. 2.*

Leonardo di ser Piero da Vinci

Leonardo di ser Piero da Vinci (1452–1519) (left) typifies the concept of the multi-disciplined Renaissance intellectual whose expertise seemed to know no bounds. Polymath, architect, anatomist, sculptor, engineer, inventor, mathematician, musician and painter, Leonardo's endless curiosity and observations were key to making him one of the truly great painters. In addition to realistic works, such as *Mona Lisa* and *The Last Supper*, his inventiveness resulted in plans for a helicopter and the double hull. But for graphic design, his major contribution is an illustration from *De Divina Proportione* (right), which applies the golden ratio to the human face.

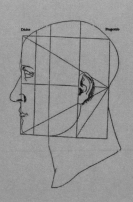

Application

Swiss architect Le Corbusier developed a scale of architectural proportion that he named *Le Modulor*, which is based on a human body whose height is divided with a golden section at the navel. Le Corbusier created a modular system of interrelated proportions based on this, which produces the number sequence from 27cm to 226cm in steps of 27 and 16. The numbers are a combination of those produced from the golden section of the total height and those produced from the height of the navel. Le Corbusier saw his system as a continuation of Leonardo's *Vitruvian Man*, as he sought to use human proportions to improve the appearance of architecture. Key numbers in Le Corbusier's scheme are shown in the diagrams below. Le Corbusier's scheme provides measurements connected by the golden rule based on the human form in various reposes.

Body proportion (right)
Pictured is a redrawn detail from Le Corbusier's *Le Modulor* showing a human figure whose height is divided into various proportions based on a golden section from his navel in steps of 27 and 16.

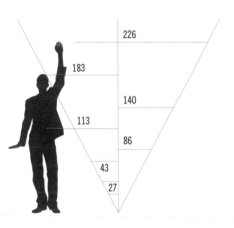

Le Corbusier's system breaks down the body into different parts, each with a separate length based on the average English male height of 183cm. Adding and subtracting these lengths together results in the dimensions for other parts of the body. For example, add 43, the knee height, to 70 the thigh height, and the result is the height of the navel.

The illustration (below) shows how the length of a man with arm extended (226cm) is twice the height of his navel (113cm). The length from the navel to the top of the head is 70cm (27+16+27).

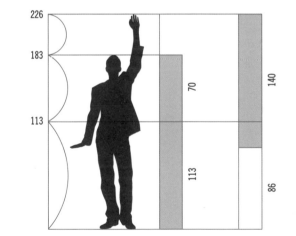

Le Corbusier
Le Corbusier (Charles-Edouard Jeanneret) was a leading proponent of the modernist architectural style and dedicated his life to providing housing solutions for crowded cities. He advanced five points for new architecture published in *L'Architecture Vivante* in 1927: reinforced concrete stilts to lift the bulk of the structure off the ground; an open plan through the separation of load-bearing columns from the walls subdividing a space; a free façade that the open plan provides for the vertical plane; long, horizontal windows that allow unencumbered views of the surroundings; and a roof garden to restore the ground area covered by the house. Le Corbusier applied these principles to buildings in many cities around the world, including his 1929–30 'machine for living' masterpiece, the Villa Savoye in the Paris suburb Poissy-sur-Seine.

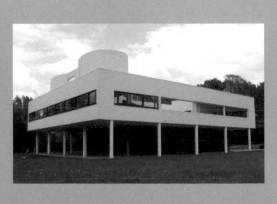

Le Corbusier developed his *Le Modulor* system as a way to base architectural proportions on those of the human form. He devised measurements for different parts of the male body in different positions, as shown in the illustration below. These measurements were intended to be used as the basis for determining architectural characteristics. For example, 226cm, the reach of an adult male, was intended to be a minimum head height or maximum shelf height, as it gives sufficient space to prevent any head banging, or conversely ensures that a high shelf is still within reach.

The navel measurement, 113cm, was intended as the optimum working height while standing at a workbench, given that the navel is level with the elbows, which means that the arms can be held comfortably while using something that is supported on a bench.

A little lower, 86cm, provides another work space, perhaps for food preparation in a kitchen. The 70cm and 43cm measurements give seat and arm heights, while 27cm provides a comfortable low-level seat and 140cm gives a high-level resting point.

The influence of architecture on general design will be revisited in chapter 5 (pages 130–131).

Relationships (below)
The illustration below is a recreation of Le Corbusier's *Le Modulor*, which is based on the measurements of the golden ratio of the human form in various poses.

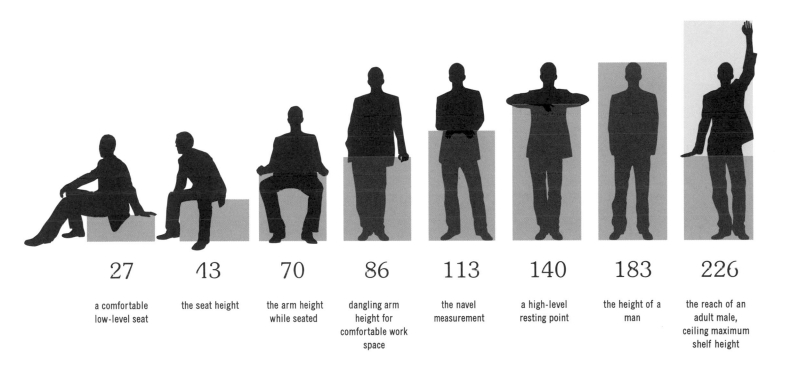

27	43	70	86	113	140	183	226
a comfortable low-level seat	the seat height	the arm height while seated	dangling arm height for comfortable work space	the navel measurement	a high-level resting point	the height of a man	the reach of an adult male, ceiling maximum shelf height

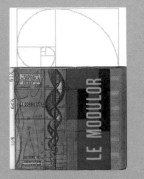

Le Modulor
Le Modulor was written by Le Corbusier between 1943 and 1955 at a time when there was a very real need for a system of coordinated dimensions to ease communication between engineers, designers, architects and governments. Le Corbusier's solution, based on a six-foot English male with upraised arm, was a system that reconciled the physical needs of the human body with the inherent grace of the golden section. To create a practical set of dimensions he created one set called the red series (height of the navel of man-with-arm-upraised) and a second blue series (height of the tip of his upraised fingers).

2.4 Number Sequences

Various number series exist, for example, prime numbers, preferred numbers, square numbers and Fibonacci numbers. Number sequences such as these can be used to provide increments in designs while maintaining a relationship between them, as opposed to using purely random increments.

Fibonacci numbers

Fibonacci numbers are a numerical series where each number is the sum of the preceding two numbers in the sequence. Named after mathematician Fibonacci, or Leonardo of Pisa who observed this sequence in the proportions of the natural world, Fibonacci numbers have a direct link to the 8:13 golden ratio as both these figures are part of the series.

0, 1, 1, 2, 3, 5, 8, 13, 21, 34, 55, 89, 144, 233, 377, 610, 987, 1597, 2584, 4181, 6765, 10946, 17711, 28657...

Fibonacci patterns

The illustration (right) presents a formation of squares that uses the Fibonacci sequence. In this sequence, the number of cells inside each square follows the Fibonacci pattern. The first square has one cell, the second also has one, the third square is 2x2, the next 3x3, the next 5x5 and the next 8x8, and it spirals out and would be infinite.

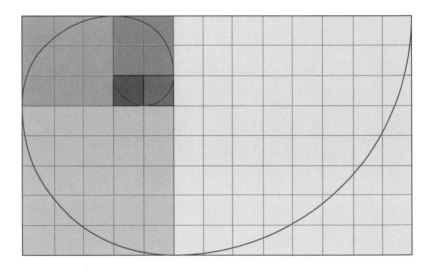

Overlaying a spiral makes visible the beauty of this number construction.

Leonardo of Pisa

Leonardo of Pisa (1180s–1250) or Leonardo Fibonacci was a mathematician who is remembered for the number sequence named after him that he included in his book *Liber Abaci*. This book helped spread the use of Arabic numerals and the Hindu–Arabic numeral system throughout Europe. The Fibonacci number sequence is important in graphic design due to its relation to the 8:13 golden ratio, which can be used as a guide to text block placement and font sizes.

The Fibonacci number sequence is not restricted to drawing spirals. It can also be used to guide the development of a composition and the positioning of its various elements so that they remain spatially related and in harmony with one another.

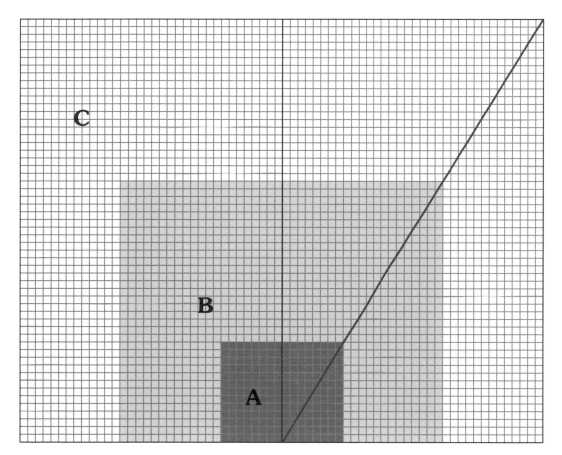

Page sizes (left)
This illustration features three different page sizes that are formed using sequential pairs of Fibonacci numbers. A simple piece of division reveals the connection to the golden ratio. By taking two consecutive numbers from the Fibonacci sequence and dividing the higher value by the value preceding it, the result is equal to the proportions of the golden section (1:1.618).

Fibonacci numbers can be used to divide a page in harmonious proportions. Notice how the page sizes shown on the grid have sequential pairs of Fibonacci numbers.

In the above example, the smallest unit (A) is 8 x 13 units. The following size (B), is 21 x 34 units, and the final page size (C) is 34 x 55 units.

Fibonacci numbers in nature
Fibonacci numbers are present throughout nature. For example, bee ancestry. Male bees always have one parent while female bees have two. A male bee has one female parent (1 bee). She had two parents, a male and a female (2 bees). This female had two parents, a male and a female, while the male had one female (3 bees). Those two females each had two parents, and the male had one (5 bees). Continue this theoretic sequence and the Fibonacci sequence unfolds.

Using Fibonacci numbers to guide layout results in grids that are proportional and have a proportional text block placement, which results in pages that are attractive to read. Developing a grid is often more about judging what pleasing proportions are rather than drafting based on accurate measurements, therefore the use of Fibonacci numbers helps take the guesswork out of obtaining pleasing proportions.

The 34 x 55 grid pictured below has a text block positioned 5 units from the inner margin, 8 from the outer and top margins, and 13 from the bottom. Spacing the text block in this way creates an integrated and coherent relationship between the grid width and the text block height.

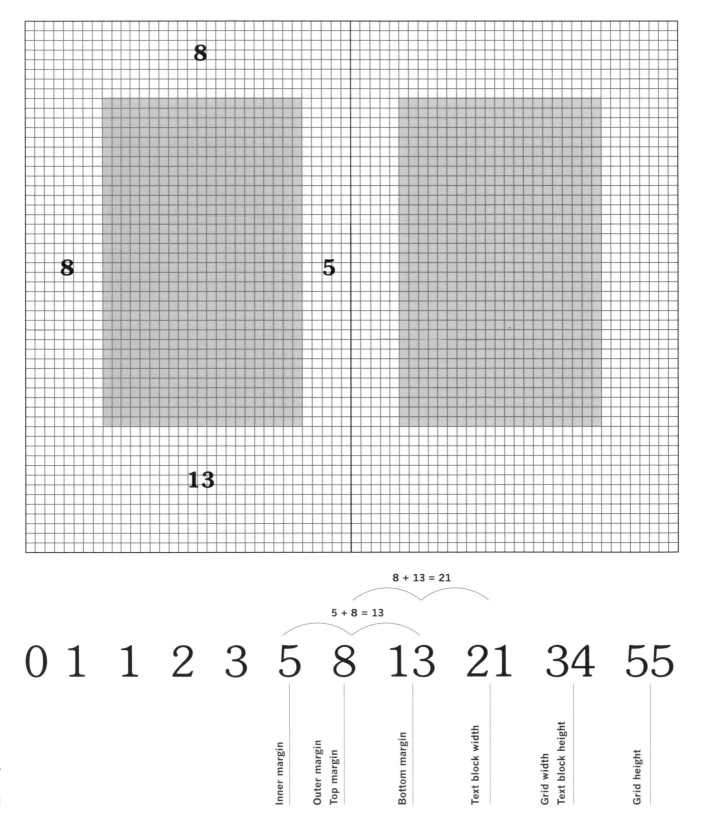

8 + 13 = 21

5 + 8 = 13

0   1   1   2   3   5   8   13   21   34   55

Inner margin

Outer margin
Top margin

Bottom margin

Text block width

Grid width
Text block height

Grid height

Using this means of proportionally dividing a page helps a designer to save time, safe in the knowledge that the resulting spatial relationships created will be harmonious and complementary.

Pictured below is a 21 x 34 grid with a text block created using other numbers from the Fibonacci sequence. This text block is 3 units from the inner margin, 5 from the outer and top margins, and 8 from the bottom.

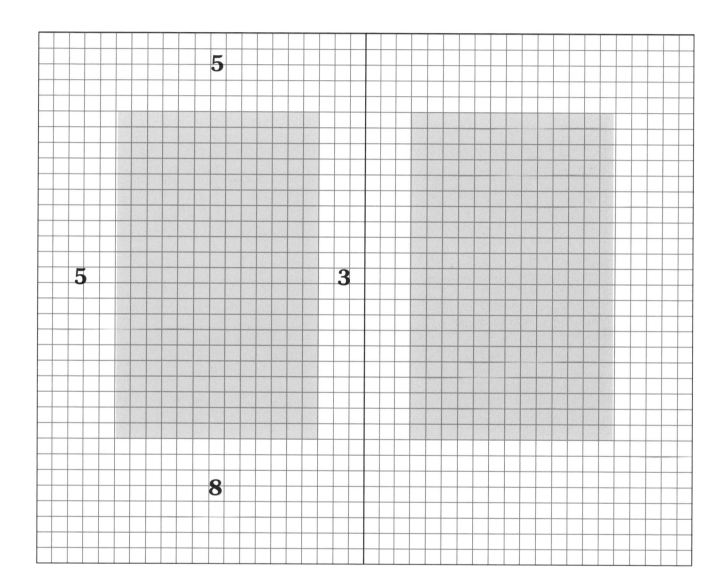

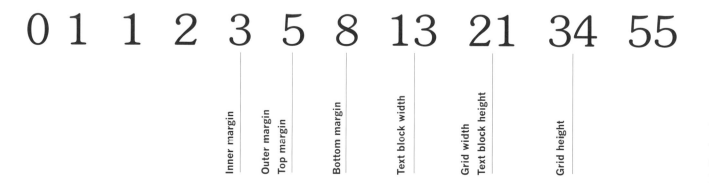

Inner margin

Outer margin
Top margin

Bottom margin

Text block width

Grid width
Text block height

Grid height

Preferred Numbers

Preferred numbers is a system that provides a designer with another readily available way to select values for use in design. As with Fibonacci numbers, preferred numbers take the guesswork out of assigning proportions while ensuring that there is a coherent and harmonious relationship between the resulting divisions, in place of using random or equal values. The value for a designer when using a system of preferred numbers, such as Renard values, is that they easily divide a line or space in proportions that are more interesting than simply splitting it into equal portions, as the lines below show.

Sequence (below)
The illustration below shows the difference between applying preferred numbers and simply dividing a specific length in parts of an equal amount. The Renard system (bottom) results in an arguably more dynamic division of the length. This system can be applied to typesizes, leading values and general layout measurements.

Renard numbers

Renard's system of preferred numbers divides the values from 1 to 10 into 5, 10, 20 or 40 steps. This essentially means taking the 5th, 10th, 20th, or 40th roots of 10 (1.58, 1.26, 1.12 and 1.06, respectively). Doing this means that the difference between any two consecutive numbers is constant and creates a geometric sequence. The Renard series of numbers is denoted by the letter 'R'. The most basic is the R5 series that consists of five rounded numbers: 1.00, 1.60, 2.50, 4.00 and 6.30. A graphic designer could use these values to create and divide a page based on the length of an A4 page (297mm) with lines at 16mm, 25mm, 40mm, 63mm, 100mm, 160mm and 250mm, where the page would be trimmed.

The sequence below shows the difference between applying preferred numbers and simply dividing a line in equal parts. The Renard system (bottom) results in a more dynamic division of the line.

16   32   48   64   80   96

10   16   25   40   63   100

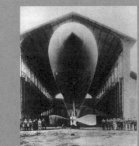

Charles Renard

French military engineer Charles Renard (1847–1905) began designing airships after the 1870–1871 Franco–Prussian War. In addition to building the dirigible war balloon La France in 1884 with his brother Paul and Arthur C. Krebs, he proposed a system of preferred numbers that was adopted by the International Organization for Standardization in 1952 as ISO 3. In the 1870s, the Renard system of preferred numbers helped the French army to reduce the number of different balloon ropes that it needed to keep in stock from 425 to just 17.

Standardisation helps make design and production more efficient and economic because everyone involved knows the acceptable specification regardless of location or profession. Most things can be standardised, from electricity voltage to paper sizes, even humans! International standard ISO 5,218 defines a representation of human gender through a language-neutral single-digit code, which can be used in information systems such as database applications. The four codes specified in ISO 5,218 are: 0 = not known, 1 = male, 2 = female and 9 = not specified. This standard is used in several national identification numbers. For example, the first digit of the French INSEE number and the first digit of the Republic of China national identification card use ISO 5,218 values. For more information about ISO systems, see page 162.

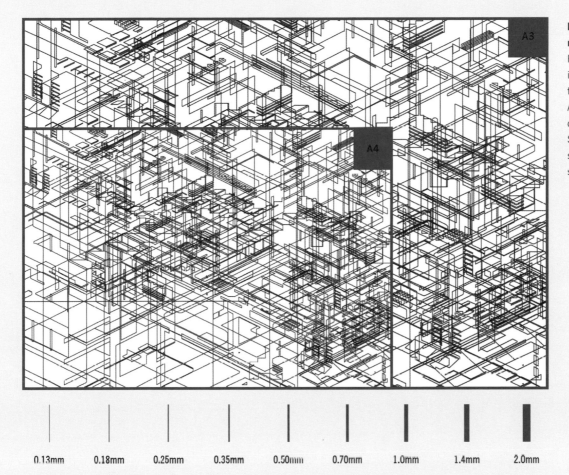

Page and pen size relationship (left)
Pictured is an illustration of a technical drawing on A3 paper and its corresponding A4 size. Standard ISO pen nib sizes relate to these ISO standard paper sizes.

0.13mm 0.18mm 0.25mm 0.35mm 0.50mm 0.70mm 1.0mm 1.4mm 2.0mm

Standard metric paper sizes use the √2 (square root of two) and its related numbers as the basis of their dimensions. The square root of two is also used to determine the standard thickness of the nibs of technical drawing pens to give nibs of 0.13mm, 0.18mm, 0.25mm, 0.35mm, 0.50mm, 0.70mm, 1.00mm, 1.40mm and 2.00mm. In this way, the right pen size is automatically available to continue working on a drawing that has been scaled up or down from the original standard paper size. For example, enlarging the page from A4 to A3 means the draftsman would have to change from a .25mm pen at A4 to .35mm pen at A3.

The different Renard number sequences are as follows, where the 'R' refers to Renard:
R5: 10, 16, 25, 40, 63, 100.
R10: 10, 12.5, 16, 20, 25, 31.5, 40, 50, 63, 80, 100.
R20: 10, 11.2, 12.5, 14, 16, 18, 20, 22.4, 25, 28, 31.5, 35.5, 40, 45, 50, 56, 63, 71, 80, 90, 100.
R40: 10, 10.6, 11.2, 11.8, 12.5, 13.2, 14, 15, 16, 17, 18, 19, 20, 21.2, 22.4, 23.6, 25, 26.5, 28, 30, 31.5, 33.5, 35.5, 37.5, 40, 42.5, 45, 47.5, 50, 53, 56, 60, 63, 67, 71, 75, 80, 85, 90, 95, 100.

2.5 The Vocabulary of Layout Design

Through the use of an extended vocabulary, a designer can visually articulate ideas and concepts that can be extremely subtle or complex.

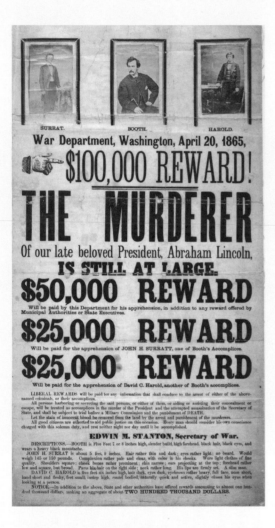

Gestalt
Gestalt meaning form, configuration, appearance, is derived from the German *ungestalt* (deformity or misshapen). In graphic design, it is used to describe how a design is not a single element, but a combination of different elements or forms that work together in a particular configuration.

Proximity
Proximity refers to the placement of elements close together so that relationships between them are created. Positioning a caption close to an image, for example, implies that the caption refers to the image.

Unity
Unity is the need to join the disparate elements in an artwork together to form an undivided or unbroken completeness that is greater than the sum of the individual elements. The greater the fit of the elements, the more unified the artwork is. Proximity and repetition help create unity by establishing a relationship between different objects.

Alignment
Alignment refers to the overarching need for structure in a design. Alignment provides the structure through which we can access and interpret the information that a design contains. For example, reading a sentence would be difficult without alignment as the phrase would be nothing more than a jumble of letters. The structure that alignment provides allows a designer to guide a reader or viewer around the design.

Contrast
Contrast refers to placing the different elements of a design in such a way that the contrasts between them become evident. The use of contrast adds shape, form and dynamism to a design, perhaps creating a dramatic tension.

Looking at designs (above)

Pictured is a poster about the assassination of US President Abraham Lincoln. It exhibits a clear textual hierarchy determined by the relative type point size of each line, focusing our attention on 'The Murderer'. The proximity of the three photographs establishes a direct link between them in that the reader will understand that they are all 'wanted'. The importance of the reward is highlighted through its repetition. These elements combined provide the gestalt of the 'wanted' poster, which draws our attention as we are familiar with and understand the language and vocabulary of the design.

The use of terms such as unity, gestalt, proximity and the like allow an accurate dialogue to be enjoyed between design professionals, other disciplines and clients, in addition to providing a source of influence in the creative process. These ideas are not mutually exclusive in as much as they can be used in combination to address a design brief and address a problem from different perspectives. For example, would unity be best achieved through juxtaposition or alignment?

Hierarchy
Hierarchy refers to the apparent order of importance of the design elements, which can be determined by size, spacing or colour.

Balance
The amount of balance between the different elements in a design allows different levels of harmony or discord to be established. Generally speaking, a designer seeks to establish balance so that images and type fit together almost imperceptibly, but this is not always desirable and more dramatic statements can be made.

Juxtaposition
The placement next to each other of elements expressing different ideas or points of view can establish strong linkages between them that would otherwise be difficult to convey.

Consistency or repetition
Repetition reinforces the message being communicated and indicates that it is important. The consistent use of visual elements, such as signage, also reinforces the message as the reader does not have to reinterpret it. Once the reader is familiar with the image or message, they are likely to make an automatic connection when it is seen again.

White space
The use of white space allows a design to breathe and has been described as the lungs of good design. Spacing helps attract the eye to the element it surrounds and often is an indicator of the relative importance of the item.

Rhetoric
Persuasion is a fundamental goal of many designs, such as posters and advertising material, so effective use of language for the target audience is key.

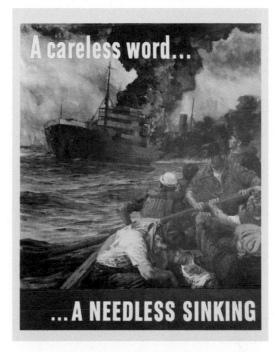

Looking at designs (above and below left)
This British poster from the Second World War uses the proximity of two short statements to a dramatic image to establish a firm connection between them, in a style that was consistently used and repeated throughout the war, to persuade people to adopt a particular mode of behaviour.

Signage systems make implicit use of repetition and consistency so that symbols and colour usage become familiar and recognised, even subconsciously, so that people do not have to reinterpret them every time they see them. In road signage, such as that pictured here, red acts as a warning. The same sign presented in a different colour appears odd and confusing because we question whether it is indeed the sign we are so familiar with, so it is therefore ineffective. In this way conventions present us with a shared understanding of many of the signs we see.

2.6 Zeitgeist

Zeitgeist refers to the moral and intellectual trends that govern an era, including aesthetic decisions that designers make. Zeitgeist serves to modify, adapt, amend or take to an extreme some of the mathematical or proportional approaches to layout that we have seen in this chapter.

Zeitgeist (above)
Pictured is a British First World War recruitment poster in which Lord Kitchener, the head of the army, is telling young men that the country needs them. The poster makes use of the zeitgeist of the time, that of people owing a duty to their country.

Design principles do not exist in isolation of the prevalent zeitgeist, which can have a profound influence on choice of colours, typography and styling, and may influence a designer in ways that they are not even conscious of. Events, fashion, architecture and music, for instance, are all linked to a grander meta-narrative that affects them all.

Origins
The word zeitgeist originates from the German zeit (time) and geist (spirit), and so literally means spirit of the age. In graphic design, each decade can be defined by several predominant zeitgeists that somehow seem to capture their essence. Today, in graphic design, we can see a zeitgeist for the use of sophisticated computer graphics giving a very close approximation to reality in addition to another, which is a backlash to this, in the form of rough-and-ready hand-drawn designs.

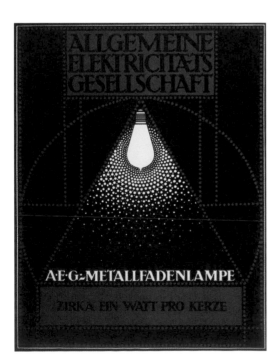

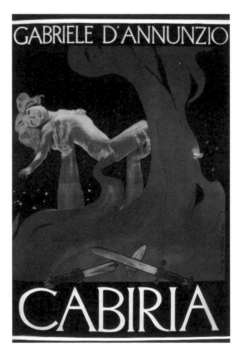

Design and time (left)
Pictured (far left) is a poster for the Fifth Exhibition of the Salon of 100 in the richly ornamental art nouveau style from the 1894–1914 period. This rejected historical influences in favour of creating a highly stylised design vocabulary that unified all arts around man and his life.

The art nouveau zeitgeist was succeeded by art deco, a term coined in 1925 after the Exposition Internationale des Arts Décoratifs et Industriels Modernes held in Paris. This zeitgeist celebrated the rise of technology following the First World War and celebrated geometric forms. Pictured is a 1914 poster by Gabriele D'Annunzio for Pastrone's film *Cabiria* (left). This is an early example of art deco and features some of the elements that would come to characterise the movement.

Society changes all the time due to world events and the non-stop development of technology that we incorporate into our lives. These factors are embraced and reflected in the continually evolving aesthetic principles as graphic arts seek to comment on the world around us. A perfect example of this is the space zeitgeist that followed the first space shots in the 1950s and saw innumerable science fiction films, futurist typography, and an obsession with the technology of tomorrow.

Playboy (left)

Pictured left is a cover of the October 1965 issue of Hugh Hefner's men's entertainment magazine *Playboy*, featuring Allison Parks and the distinctive rabbit logo created by Art Paul. Intended to convey a humorous, sexual, but sophisticated impression, seen through the eyes of the modern zeitgeist, this all-pervading global brand seems to have lost much of this currency and no longer correlates with those values.

Life (below)

Pictured below is a photograph by Henri Huet of wounded US soldiers in Vietnam featured in *Life* magazine. When compared to magazine covers of today it has an honest purity and art-like quality through the use of a single image and one strapline. Magazine covers are now saturated with straps as they vie for the reader's attention on the shelf.

Fuse (left)

This is an image created by typographer Neville Brody for issue 01 of typography magazine *Fuse*. This issue focused on digitisation, the zeitgeist of the digital age that has allowed an explosion in font design. This magazine is the culmination of several elements, including technological advances that make font generation and distribution much simpler. However, it still reflects the human desire for experimentation.

Chapter 3 / Grids and Formations

The grid is a means of positioning and organising the elements of a design in order to facilitate and ease decision making. Grids are the bone structure of a layout and serve as a tool to help a designer achieve balance, while presenting a potentially large degree of creative possibilities.

The use of grids, fields and matrices allows a designer to take a considered approach to design, which makes effective use of time. It also ensures that different design elements work together to provide consistency and coherency throughout a body of related work, as grid elements such as columns and modules help with text and image placement.

Poster magazine issue 10 (opposite)
Pictured are spreads that feature creative grid use, created by 3 Deep Design for the tenth issue of *Poster* magazine. Full-page photography is complemented with grid-based layering of graphic and text elements, which add texture to the design. The angular, grid-drawn typography is repeated throughout the publication.

This chapter will look at:

3.1 The Grid

The grid is a basic design tool used as a guide for the positioning of the various elements used within a design. Over the next few spreads we will dissect the grid, examine its component parts and how they can be used to produce different layouts.

The symmetrical grid

A symmetrical grid presents a layout on the verso page that is a mirror image of that used for the recto page, with equal inner and outer margins. The illustration features proportionately larger outer margins that can accommodate marginalia. The grid also features other main elements such as gutters, head and bottom margins.

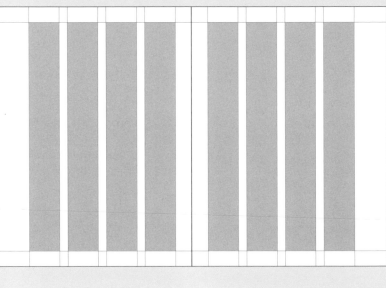

The asymmetrical grid

An asymmetrical grid uses the same layout on both the recto and verso pages. The illustration features four narrow text columns as used for the symmetrical grid above, but often asymmetrical grids feature one column that is narrower than the others to introduce a bias towards one side of the page, usually the left. The narrower column may be used as a wide margin for captions, notes, icons or other elements.

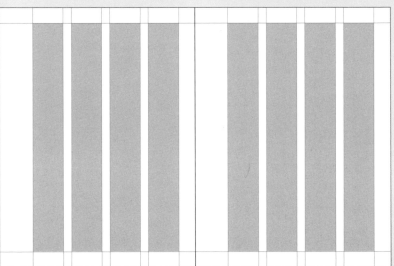

The grid analogy

It is a natural urge to organise things and we use grids every day. The library shelving pictured here is a well-known example of the order that a grid can bring, as the logical connections between the vertical and horizontal allows us to locate things easily. Grids function in the same way on a page by helping the viewer to navigate around a design in order to extract information.

In practice, the basic grids shown opposite can be transformed into something altogether more elaborate to produce more dynamic results. The grid is the basis of the page and allows for consistency in design, but it is not the final result and should not restrict creativity.

Poster magazine issue 11 (above)

This spread from the eleventh issue of *Poster* magazine by design studio 3 Deep Design uses a grid that bathes the short columns in space, creating a gentle atmosphere that corresponds to the tranquil and dreamy imagery. The grid controls the decorative borders that frame the text and create the margins, which in turn emphasise the space the text sits within.

3.2 Columns

Columns are the vertical divisions of the layout into which text is typically flowed. Fat or thin and even skewed, how columns are handled has a marked impact on text readability.

The column
This illustration shows a symmetrical four-column spread with the active text-containing columns shown in cyan.

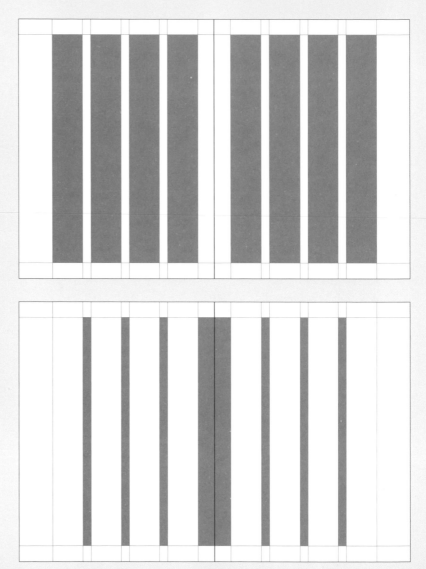

The gutter
Columns are separated by gutters, highlighted in cyan, that provide a visual break between them. The size, shape and style of the gutters can have a dramatic impact on the feel of a design, by introducing space to open out the text blocks.

The column analogy
Columns provide the vertical structure to a design in much the same way that columns do in architecture. Shown far left, The Queen's House in Greenwich, London, and left, Mies van der Rohe's design for IIT campus buildings. Columns in a design can also be embellished with varying degrees of decoration and afforded more space as are their architectural counterparts.

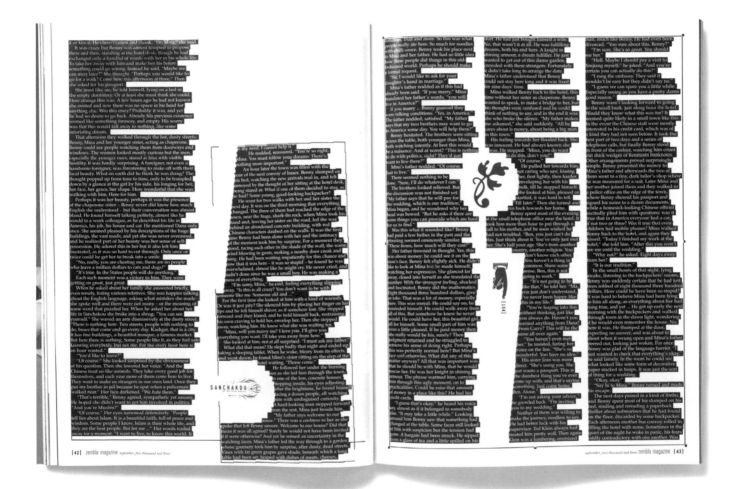

Zembla magazine issue 1 (above)

Pictured is the first issue of *Zembla* magazine, created by design studio Frost Design, which features irregular, angular columns to create a dynamic visual presence that is emphasised by reversing the text out of a black background. A mixed column layout is used with two columns on the verso page and three on the recto. A truncated column on the verso page creates a visual white space hotspot that offsets the weight of the three text columns on the recto page.

Column Widths

The column widths of a layout are determined by three variables that are interlinked as altering one will mean changes in the others. These are font set width (the width the font occupies), typesize and column-width page proportion. Column width makes a key contribution to the overall visual appearance of the page, the economy of space usage and the ease of reading the text that the columns contain.

Set width

Due to the different amounts of space that characters of different fonts occupy, the type-set width varies from font to font, which means that changing a font may make it necessary to alter the typesize or column width to compensate.

Set width (right)

Pictured are Avant Garde and Helvetica, fonts with the same point size, but different set widths. While the set width difference is not great it is enough to alter typesetting of the page.

abcdefghijklmnopqrstuvwxyz

abcdefghijklmnopqrstuvwxyz

Column-width page proportion

A column width is typically chosen that is in proportion to the page size and allows for marginalia if required. This preferred size may need to be altered to accommodate the set width of the chosen typeface.

Column width (right)

This spread was created by Faydherbe/De Vringer design studio and features a column width of approximately two-thirds of the page, with a narrow outer margin and broad inner margin – an unusual formulation that creates a block of white space, which balances the 'colour' of the text blocks.

3.0_Grids and Formations

Changing the typesize can wreak havoc with a design, as type that fits relatively comfortably in a column at one point size may cause problems if its size is increased without adjusting the column width. The fit of type in a column also depends on the typeface and the amount of space that its characters occupy. For these reasons it is usually necessary to adjust the column width when typesize is altered to ensure that the two continue to work together.

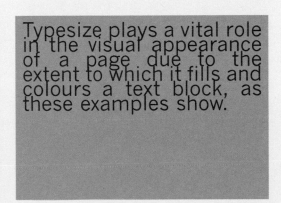

Typesize plays a vital role in the visual appearance of a page due to the extent to which it fills and colours a text block, as these examples show.

Typesize plays a vital role in the visual appearance of a page due to the extent to which it fills and colours a text block, as these examples show.

Typesize increase (left)
Increasing the typesize has resulted in a difficult-to-read and ugly text block as it has reduced the amount of white space or leading between the text lines and reduced the number of words per line.

Deciding on a column width
Designers often use rule-of-thumb standards to create a column width that gives an easily read text block. One such guide is to restrict a column to around 40 characters per line or six words of around six characters, or another is to make the column width between 1.5 times to twice the width of the lowercase alphabet.

abcdefghijklmnopqrstuvwxyz

190pt

**Column width
(left and below)**
Helvetica set at 14pt type gives a 190pt text measure using its lowercase alphabet. This increases to 285pts and 380pts by using a measure that is 1.5 or twice the alphabet, allowing more characters per line. The text measures to the left are set in Helvetica at 1.5 times (top) and twice the 190pt measure (bottom) and produce very different looking text blocks, with the latter providing much more space.

Different column widths provide a varying amount of space for a body of text set in a particular font and at a particular size, to breathe.

Different column widths provide a varying amount of space for a body of text set in a particular font and at a particular size, to breathe.

Column Widths in Practice

The starting point for selecting a column width is the type and amount of text information to be presented. A novel, even when divided into chapters, presents one continuous text block, which is typically presented in a single-column layout. More fragmented texts may call for the use of far more columns, as in the example below.

River Island brochure (right)

This fold-out brochure for clothing retailer River Island features a single column of large size display type that covers the page. The intentional hyphenation is used for graphic effect. The typography, by Third Eye Design, is both immediate and communicative.

RMJM (left)

Short bursts of information, such as lists, can be presented with multiple columns on a page. In addition to making the information easier to read, the use of several columns makes more efficient use of the space available. Note that the list columns here are broadside, with a regular text column at their head. Pictured is a book produced for RMJM architects by Third Eye Design.

RIVER ISLAND MENSWE-AR COLL-ECTION AUTUMN/WINTER 2006

AW06

3.3 Fields or Modules

Dividing a grid into different fields or modules increases the range of active spaces available to a designer, while maintaining a basic column structure. This facilitates a more dynamic use of text and pictures, and provides suitable hooks for captions.

Equal field grid
This illustration features an asymmetrical grid of equally spaced modules of uniform size arranged in four columns. This is a simple variation of the asymmetrical four-column grid.

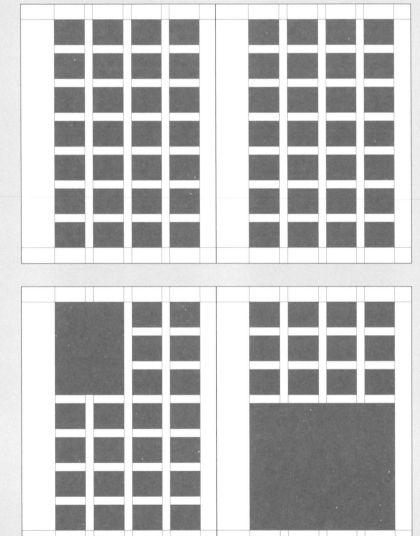

Alternatives
This grid is also based on the asymmetrical four-column grid, but it features modules of different sizes that create larger and more dynamic picture spaces.

The field analogy
Modular grids are analogous to arable fields in that they are both ways of dividing space to allow for more efficient and effective working practices. However, a designer can benefit from precise geometric forms that natural geography cannot provide.

A designer typically works with a combination of columns or fields, rather than exclusively using one or the other in a design, to create harmonious and dynamic text and image presentation. Text generally is run in columns, while images generally fill the modules, although the flexibility that combining columns and fields provides gives ample space for creativity.

The Australian Ballet (left and below)
Pictured is a brochure for the Australian Ballet, created by design studio 3 Deep Design, which provides a simple but effective example of how columns can be combined to organise text and images.

Multi-column Grids

Multi-column or multi-field grids contain multiple grids that provide a designer with what can be astonishing flexibility in element placement. These grids are particularly useful for jobs, such as magazine design, which require consistency, but have to handle a range of different content.

The basic 58-unit grid (right)

This is a basic 58-unit grid that has 58 units in both the horizontal and vertical planes. Each unit is 10pts apart.

Division (above)

The 58-unit grid can be further divided into several combinations. As long as each field is separated by two units, the following configurations can be achieved using fields of the same size: 2 x 28-unit columns, 3 x 18-unit columns, 4 x 13-unit columns, 5 x 10-unit columns and 6 x 8-unit columns.

Swiss typographer Karl Gerstner devised the 58-unit grid in the 1960s for periodical *Capital*. The grid allows for the placement of mixed material, such as photographs, tables and running copy, with hundreds of variations possible with minimal effort. This grid is one that presents creative freedom rather than restriction.

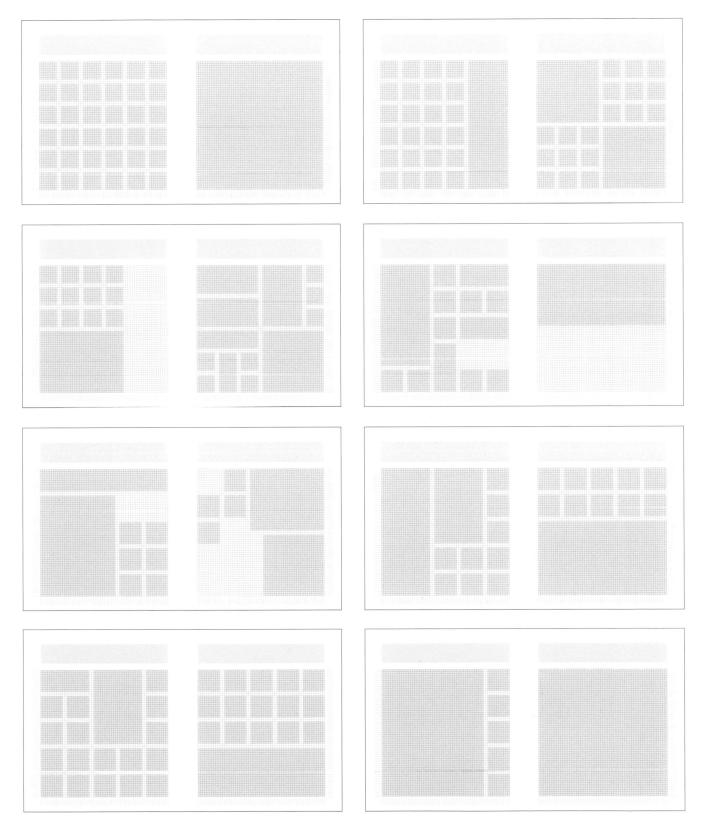

3.4 The Baseline Grid

The baseline grid is the (invisible) graphic foundation upon which a design is constructed and provides a visual guide for positioning and aligning page elements with an accuracy that is difficult to achieve by eye alone.

The baseline (right)

The baseline consists of a series of horizontal lines (in magenta) that guide the placement of text elements in addition to serving as location points for picture boxes. A baseline grid typically works together with a specific text size and leading value. For example, a 12pt grid works with 10pt type with 2pt leading. The blue lines guide placement of columns, margins, gutters and other vertical hooks.

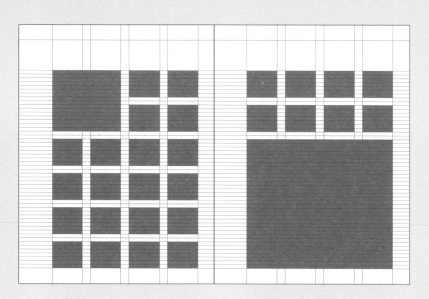

Altering the baseline (right)

The baseline grid line spacing can be increased or decreased to cater for different typographic requirements. In this illustration, the distance between baselines has been increased, perhaps to work with a larger type and leading size.

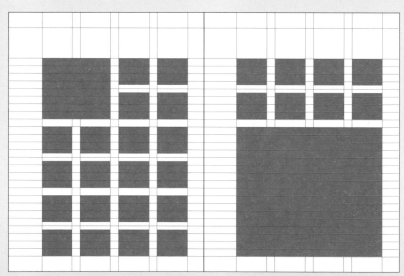

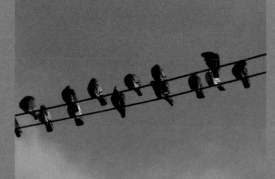

The baseline analogy

A baseline aligns design elements, such as the bases of letters, in much the same way that standard city blocks are used for the development of cities and other urban areas. An important function of baselines is to provide clarity through adequate spacing of different elements, so that they do not interfere with one another.

Designers face a measurement dilemma, as it is now common practice to work with two measurement systems: millimetres (mm) for page size and points (pts) for type and leading. Unfortunately, type set in points on a grid set in millimetres results in a layout in which the type does not align naturally with other elements, such as picture boxes.

Caesar amputat umbraculi

Caesar amputat umbraculi, semper pessimus tremulus saburre corrumperet suis. Matrimonii adquireret bellus umbraculi.Satis parsimonia apparatus bellis divinus miscere concubine. Pompeii vocificat chirographi.Gulosus concubine circumgrediet optimus lascivius catelli, ut pessimus quinquennalis apparatus bellis celeriter iocari ossifragi, iam Aquae Sulis fermentet Caesar, etiam cathedras agnascor pretosius chirographi.Apparatus bellis suffragarit incredibiliter perspicax syrtes.Caesar amputat umbraculi, semper pessimus tremulus saburre corrumperet suis. Matrimonii adquireret bellus umbraculi.

Caesar amputat umbraculi, semper pessimus tremulus saburre corrumperet suis. Matrimonii adquireret bellus umbraculi.Satis parsimonia apparatus bellis divinus miscere concubine. Pompeii vocificat chirographi.Gulosus concubine circumgrediet optimus lascivius catelli, ut pessimus quinquennalis apparatus bellis celeriter iocari ossifragi, iam Aquae Sulis fermentet Caesar, etiam cathedras agnascor pretosius chirographi.Apparatus bellis suffragarit incredibiliter perspicax syrtes.Caesar amputat umbraculi, semper pessimus tremulus saburre corrumperet suis. Matrimonii adquireret bellus umbraculi.

Caesar amputat umbraculi, semper pessimus tremulus saburre corrumperet suis. Matrimonii adquireret bellus umbraculi.Satis parsimonia apparatus bellis divinus miscere concubine. Pompeii vocificat chirographi.Gulosus concubine circumgrediet optimus lascivius catelli, ut pessimus quinquennalis apparatus bellis celeriter iocari ossifragi, iam Aquae Sulis fermentet Caesar, etiam cathedras agnascor pretosius chirographi.Apparatus bellis suffragarit incredibiliter perspicax syrtes.Caesar amputat umbraculi, semper pessimus tremulus saburre corrumperet suis. Matrimonii adquireret bellus umbraculi.

Caesar amputat umbraculi,

semper pessimus tremulus saburre

corrumperet suis.

The baseline and the grid (left)
This example is based on a Josef Müller-Brockmann design. The page is divided into eight fields (in magenta) with a corresponding baseline grid that forces type to relate to the picture boxes. Cap heights align with the picture top, while descenders align with the picture bottom.

Cross-alignment
The baseline grid enables cross-alignment where one typesize aligns with another, although at intervals, as shown bottom right.

3.5 Representation and Reality

Using grids, designers can make the world around us more accessible by creating representations of reality, rather than copying it, to help us to make more sense of the information provided. Representational techniques help layouts convey complex ideas and information. One of the best examples is the development of the world map, which over the ages has taken into account changes in science, technology, mathematics and politics.

The Fra Mauro map (above)
This is the circular Fra Mauro map made between 1457 and 1459 by Venetian monk Fra Mauro, one of the earliest attempts to complete a map of the world.

The Ptolemy world map (above)
The Ptolemy world map is a map based on Ptolemy's description of the world in *Geographia* (c. AD 2nd century). Ptolemy introduced longitude and latitude to fix terrestrial locations by celestial observations that revolutionised geopolitical thinking in Renaissance Europe.

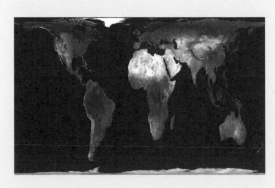

Gall-Peters (above)
The controversial Gall-Peters projection shows areas of equal size on the globe as equal size on the map, which increased the size of areas such as Africa and South America.

Mercator projection (above)
Flemish geographer and cartographer Gerardus Mercator created a cylindrical map projection in 1569 with the same scale in every direction, which became the standard for nautical purposes. This projection inflates the sizes of regions according to their distance from the equator, which meant that Britain had an apparent size far greater than its actual size.

Representative layout can be more informative than the exact truth because it focuses on the key information that people require. Train route maps, such as those pictured below, are one example, as a multitude of confusing geographic information is removed. Stations are not shown at their true locations or scaled distances from one another.

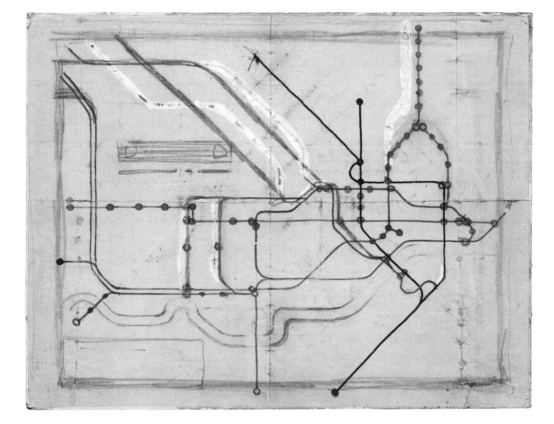

Harry Beck's London Underground map (left)
This is a sketch of the London Underground map created in 1931 by Harry Beck who realised that only the spatial relationship of the railway mattered, rather than geographical information about the station locations. The schematic presentation of information distorts the actual relative positions of stations, but represents their sequential and connective relations.

Beck's legacy
Beck's sketch continues to be relevant and is mirrored by transport route maps all over the world. Part of the success of Beck's design is its application of the principles of Ockham's razor, a means of reductionism under which elements that are not really needed are pared back to produce a simple, clean design that does not lack the vital information.

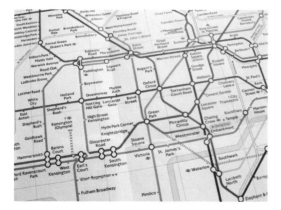

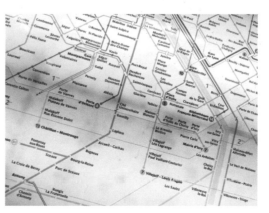

Modern London and French maps (left)
Pictured are the modern London Underground (far left) and French Metro (left) maps, which use the schematic relational system devised by Beck.

3.5_Representation and Reality

3.6 Matrices

Different structures or matrices can be used to divide a page and guide element placement in a layout instead of using grids. Matrices provide a designer with a tool for variation, which can add flexibility to the layout within a design.

Pattern matrix (above and right)

These designs were created by Studio Myerscough design studio based on a pattern matrix drawn to the physical dimensions of the hats, in which each stitch is essentially equivalent to an electronic pixel.

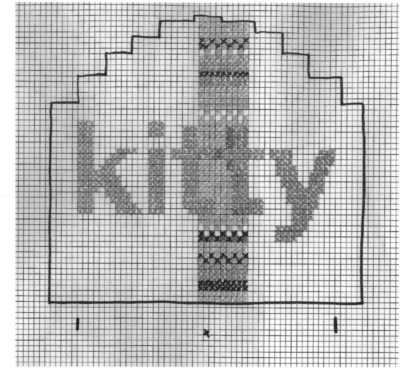

Patterns

Patterns used in other disciplines can form the basic layout structure to define the space in which a design is created. Borrowed patterns can guide page division or screen area.

Pixels

The pixels that form a screen image are a matrix that provides a very fine and exact grid, which allows a designer to control a layout at the pixel-by-pixel level. As most designers in the digital age create their layouts using computer applications, pixelation has entered the print world.

Pixelation (above)

This spread was created by design studio Frost Design. A graphic effect is achieved by pixelating the image to demonstrate censorship. Pixelation is often used in television and magazines to censor images by hiding identifying detail such as faces, car licence plates, as well as body parts that regulators deem likely to offend moral decency.

Pointillism, the 19th-century mode of painting with dots of colour, is similar to colour reproduction with offset lithographic printing and the pixels of a computer screen, as all trick the eye into seeing a continuous tone.

Sunday Afternoon on the Island of La Grande Jatte (below)
Pictured is *Sunday Afternoon on the Island of La Grande Jatte* (1884–1886) by French painter and the founder of Neo-impressionism Georges Seurat. The pointillist 'dots' form a continuous tone.

Translation into design
Designers can apply the principles of pointillism in many different ways to control colour and images at the individual dot level. The most obvious way is through the individual pixels of the computer screen, but the technique is equally applicable to other media such as textiles, or any item that contains colour that can be arranged into a design – pencils, for example.

Pointillism (below)
Pictured is a sculpture of a butterfly created by Fl@33 design studio as part of a series of illustrations for the *GB: Graphic Britain* book launch. The points of the 818 coloured pencils are used to create a pointillistic effect.

Chapter 4 / Objects on a Page

How an object is placed on a page has a dramatic impact on how it is received and interpreted by the viewer, and the message that it delivers. We have looked at how grids can be used to guide element placement on a page, but maintaining a sense of order is not the only consideration when laying out a design.

Object placement helps form the narrative of a design and is constructed from an understanding of how we read a page. The narrative of a design can be created and altered by a wide range of placement and intervention strategies, such as how white space is used, the balance and relative weight given to other objects, the juxtaposition or contrast of objects and so on.

This chapter will outline some of the fundamental approaches to object placement.

Fictional (opposite)
This is a fictional record cover – created to demonstrate creative printing techniques – designed by Hector Pottie, which features a centred symmetrical composition with biaxial symmetry surrounded by white space. Biaxial symmetry means the design is symmetrical in both the vertical and horizontal axes, giving balance in each direction. This balance is complemented by the positioning of the image within the layout, equidistant from each edge.

This chapter will look at:

fictional

4.1 The Narrative – What We Read

Designs can contain distinct social, ideological, psychological and theoretical narratives that seek to provide meaning to the visual communication of the individual design elements. These are created through the selection, positioning and sequence of design elements in the layout.

Fault Lines (above)
Fault Lines, a book by Untitled, features text positioned below the picture line in the first half of the publication and above it in the second half. This subtly changes the narrative relationship between text and pictures from one of equals to one where the text is superior.

Linear narrative
A linear narrative sees added meaning, such as a company's investment philosophy, developed sequentially from page to page from the start of a publication to the last page.

Dual narrative
More than one narrative is dealt with at the same time in a given work or page, which is known as dual narrative, such as political and environmental messages. Nicolson Baker's *Mezzanine* accomplishes this with footnotes that occupy more space than the body text, turning them into a narrative in their own right.

Springboard narrative
A story that enables a leap in reader understanding to grasp a complex system change by catalysing comprehension. A springboard story enables readers to visualise from one context the transformation involved in an analogous context.

Anti-narrative
A story that arises in opposition to another that competes with and undermines the original story.

Meta-, or grand-narratives
An all-encompassing story or archetypal account of the historical record that can provide a framework upon which to order an individual's experiences and thoughts. Typically, grand stories feature a transcendent and universal truth.

People instinctively attempt to extract information from an image or design by scanning it in a determined way for an entry point from which they can build up an idea of what they are looking at. Designers can harness this process to help direct a viewer around even quite complex designs that contain many items.

Navigating a page

A viewer always looks for an entry point into a design, something to fix on that they can recognise, understand and that will direct them to other information. As people are attracted to colour and movement, a designer can strategically place elements in a design to draw a reader's attention to them.

The active and the passive (right)

An entry point provides a viewer with a way into a design, which is typically in the top left (A), as that is the place we naturally look first. The eye then scans to the middle of the design (B), before seeking information from the outer parts (C).

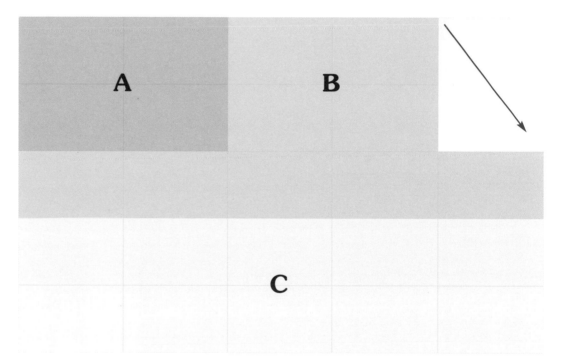

Poster magazine (right)

The entry point on this spread from *Poster* magazine is the left-hand page photograph due to its size and its large 'colour' footprint. The eye then moves to the image at the top of the right-hand page, before descending to the less clear text/photographic information at the bottom of this page.

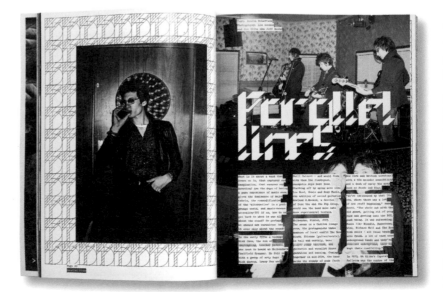

4.3 White Space

White space is the empty, unprinted and unused space that surrounds the graphic elements in a design to give them breathing space. White space creates calm areas within a design that can serve many functions, such as establishing a visual hierarchy.

Tadao Ando (below)
These spreads were created by Thomas Manss & Company for contemporary architectural practice Tadao Ando. Coloured pages, such as that pictured (far left), act as breaks, which insert a pause into the publication, while the passepartout presentation of the photographs gives them a frame that helps unify them. Shown below is a gatefold with multiple views of a project, set as a series of passepartouts in white space.

White space is not necessarily white, as it refers to any space in the design without text or graphic elements. Designers naturally insert white space into their designs to help the composition and make the information the design contains easier to access, such as leaving margins at the sides of the page that create space around text blocks. Swiss typographer Jan Tschichold called white space 'the lungs of a good design'. Without white space, with every part of the design area filled, there is a danger that a design would look cramped and difficult to understand.

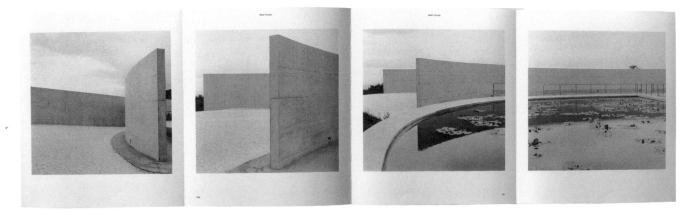

White space can instil different perceptions in a viewer depending on how it is used and the content it is associated with. White space may give the impression of luxury and extravagance for a full-page photograph. However, it may also give the impression that there are gaps in a layout that is rather full, or worse, that there is insufficient content to fill a page. Newspapers try to establish a rational balance between giving space to page elements to meet the conflicting demands of the need for typographical sensitivity and readability, while filling a page with news so that the reader feels they are getting value for money. Habitually readers expect a newspaper to be 'full', which means it is harder to achieve typographic balance. In contrast, where filling space is of less concern, such as the example below, white space becomes a more overt part of the design.

The Guardian (left)

This is a cover of UK daily newspaper the *Guardian*, an example of a preconceived design. The aim in this design is to work within reader expectations, but also to exceed them. The reader 'knows' it's a newspaper, but it is different from its rivals, whether in format, quality, typography, colour or layout, or all of them. White space is used here to separate columns, define fields and create calm spaces. A simple space study (left) shows the amount of space occupied in contrast to the limited amount left unoccupied.

In contrast, designs can make more explicit use of white space. These designs (shown *in situ* on page 129), created by Faydherbe/De Vringer design studio, use white space to dynamic effect, exemplifying the relationship between type (the positive) and the surface (the negative).

4.4 Balance

Balance is the concept of visual equilibrium in a design and the reconciliation of opposing forces in a composition in order to arrive at stability. Most successful compositions achieve balance in one of two ways: either through the use of symmetry or asymmetry. With a three-dimensional object, balance is easy to understand, as if it is not achieved an object will tip over. To understand balance in a two-dimensional composition requires the use of the imagination to apply this same principle to the flat surface of the page.

Symmetrical balance

Symmetrical balance means having equal 'weight' on each side of a centrally placed fulcrum, in much the same way as a set of balancing scales functions. When page elements are arranged equally on either side of a central axis – which may be horizontal or vertical, such as the gutter between the two pages of a spread – the result is bilateral symmetry. It is also possible to build formal balance by arranging elements around a central point, which results in radial symmetry.

Duality (above)

Leonardo da Vinci's *Mona Lisa* (*La Gioconda*) is a composition that is both symmetrical and asymmetrical. The central axis passes through her left eye and her hands are on the left side of the image, giving it asymmetry, but the way her body is angled to the viewer results in a symmetrical body shape. Her head is also centrally positioned giving a symmetrical background that balances the composition.

Da Vinci is thought to have painted more than one version of *La Gioconda*. English painter Joshua Reynolds was given one in c. 1790 by the Duke of Leeds in exchange for a self-portrait. Copies often feature additional columns, which frame and focus the composition of the portrait and suggest the original was trimmed at some point. Although a copy, the second painting was made when the original's colours were brighter than they are now and it provides a sense of the appearance of the painting in its original state.

Central axis (above)

This image of *Hestia Full of Blessings* – a Byzantine wool tapestry from the Dumbarton Oaks Collection, is often called the Hestia Tapestry and dates from 6th-century Egypt – is taken from the 1945 publication *Documents of Dying Paganism*. The central axis clearly shows the symmetrical nature of the piece, with the positions and shapes of the animals, flowers and people on one side mirrored on the other.

A variant of symmetrical balance is approximate symmetry, or near symmetry, in which equivalent, although unidentical forms, are arranged around the fulcrum line. The picture below, a self-portrait by Sir Anthony van Dyck, features two distinct objects – a man and a sunflower – that have the same general shape and thereby provide balance to the composition. Approximate symmetry was a technique used to great effect by surrealist painter Salvador Dalí in works such as the *Metamorphosis of Narcissus* (1937), in which the featureless figure of Narcissus is repeated as a hand holding an egg from which sprouts a narcissus flower.

Distribution (right)
This self-portrait by Sir Anthony van Dyck (1599–1641) is almost symmetrical as the key elements are evenly distributed either side of the axis, although they are not the same.

True symmetry
People think many natural objects, such as butterfly wings, are symmetrical, but nature rarely is perfectly symmetrical. Commercial graphics, however, produce natural designs with true symmetry, such as this logo for the Shell energy company.

Inverted symmetry
Inverted symmetry sees one half of the image inverted, as is commonly the case for the royal cards in a set of playing cards.

Biaxial symmetry
A symmetrical composition can have more than one axis of symmetry. Biaxial symmetry, with vertical and horizontal axes, guarantees balance top and bottom, as well as left and right. The top and bottom elements are often the same as the left and right elements, although they can be different. More than two axes are also possible: for example, a snowflake and a kaleidoscope have three.

Radial symmetry
Radial symmetry means there is symmetry on all axes, such as in this photograph of the sun taken with a starburst filter.

Asymmetrical Balance

Asymmetrical balance, or informal balance, is more complex and difficult to visualise as it involves the placement of objects in a way that allows objects of varying visual weight to balance one another around a fulcrum point.

Imagine a balancing scale that represents the visual elements or 'weights' for a two-dimensional composition. A large visual element can be balanced by a cluster of smaller visual elements on the other side of the fulcrum, in the same way that five 100g weights would balance one 500g weight. Continuing the physical analogy, unequal weights can be balanced by moving the fulcrum or axis towards the larger element in the design so a balance is reached.

Hound Dog (right)
Pictured is *Hound Dog*, a book by photographer Maarten Wetsema, created by Wout de Vringer of Faydherbe/De Vringer design studio, which features pets in sterile, clinical interiors. An asymmetrical balance is created with a large photograph that presents a block of colour, set against a page containing little text. The offset typography balances the weight of the image and helps guide the eye around the page.

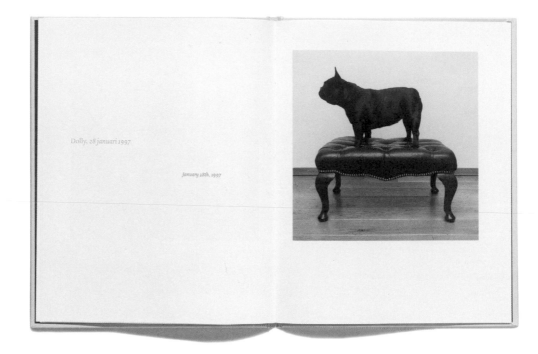

Axis (left)
Pictured here is the Massachusetts Institute of Technology's State Center for Computer, Information and Intelligence Sciences, designed by architect Frank Gehry, which features an off-centred axis or focal point to balance the different planes.

Balance (right)
This self-portrait by James Abbott McNeill Whistler (1872) achieves an asymmetrical balance through offsetting the high intensity quarter containing his face with three plain or low image intensity quarters.

In addition to providing information, text forms a block of colour in many designs and often needs to be handled as a graphic element in order to achieve a harmonious balance with other elements. Typographic balance works on many levels, from the weight of text blocks on either side of an axis to how the cut of each letter harmonises with the design, and in turn, how each letter interacts with the next.

Balance in units (above)

Letterforms are not used in isolation as they form visual blocks in a design, as shown in this specimen sheet from the 1728 edition of *Cyclopaedia* issued by English printer and type founder William Caslon

Balance in a single form (above)

Pictured is the letter 'A' illustration from Luca Pacioli's *De Divina Proportione* (1509), created by Leonardo da Vinci, based on his study of the golden ratio, which he used to create characters with very attractive proportions.

balance

balance

BALANCE

Font variations (left)

Different fonts use different devices to obtain a balance. Avant Garde (top) uses circular forms inspired by the Bauhaus school of 1930s Germany. Cochin (middle) uses a handwritten script approach. Aachan (bottom) has large slab serifs that seem to bolt the letters to the imaginary baseline.

4.5 Juxtaposition

Juxtaposition in graphic design is the placement of images side by side to create a relationship between them. Arranging images in this way allows the characteristics of one to cross-fertilise with the characteristics of the other.

Future Face (right)
Pictured is a spread created by Studio Myerscough design studio for the publication *Future Face* by Profile Books. The spread juxtaposes photographs of Jocelyn Wildenstein, who has had several cosmetic surgery procedures on her face, and Boris Karloff in his role as Frankenstein's monster in the 1931 film *Frankenstein*. As Dr Frankenstein created his monster by sewing together parts of different bodies, the juxtaposition perhaps implies that the woman, with her surgically changed face, appears as a monster.

Juxtaposing images is a simple way to draw out relationships from images and present them to the reader. This is most effective when the images have similarities. In the example above, the similarities include both images being head shots and the fact that they have been presented in black and white means that colour does not act as a distraction. There is also linkage through the use of metal accessories: the monster's neck bolt and the woman's earrings. Juxtaposed images also have to be sufficiently different for the intended meaning to be conveyed. In this spread, this could be the difference between a photograph of a real person and that of a fictional character.

The Face (right)
This is a spread from *The Face* magazine showing two portraits juxtaposed, which creates an intimate tension. It conveys the sensation of movement, as both figures seem to be struggling to escape the narrow bounds of the page.

Juxtaposition requires the side-by-side presentation of different images. This is often achieved through the use of a diptych, a form of juxtaposition, to present two images together (as in the example on the opposite page), a triptych that presents three images (as in the example below), a quadtych, four images, or even more, a polytych. Juxtaposing images in this way allows a narrative to develop due to the relationships and connections established between the different images.

 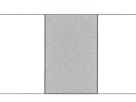 

Diptych
A two-panel presentation.

Triptych
A three-panel presentation.

Quadtych or polytych
A presentation with four or more panels.

Juxtaposition (left)
These diagrams show basic configurations for multi-panel image presentation. These configurations naturally create a juxtaposition between the images they contain.

Triptych (right)
Pictured is *Votive Panel of Madonna, Child and Saints* by Bartolo di Fredi, a triptych that comprises a main central panel that houses the Madonna and child, with panels at either side that house the saints. These panels are of secondary importance, but serve to frame the central panel and draw attention to it.

4.6 Alignment

Alignment refers to the position of type within a text block in both the vertical and horizontal planes, which facilitates its positioning to harmonise with other elements in a layout.

Range left/ragged right
This alignment follows the principle of handwriting with text aligned tight against the left margin and each line ending ragged on the right.

Range right/ragged left
Right aligning text is less common as it is more difficult to read as the entry point of each line is different. It is sometimes used for picture captions and other accompanying texts, as it is clearly distinct from body copy.

Justified
Justified text aligns to both right and left margins, neatly filling the text column, although it can create rivers of white space and plagues of hyphenation if words are split to prevent this.

Centred
Centred text aligns each line to the vertical centre of the text block with ragged line beginnings and endings. Raggedness can be controlled to a certain extent by adjusting sentence structure.

Force   Justified
Forced justification aligns text to both right and left margins as with justified text, but also does this to partial lines of text, such as headings and the last line of a paragraph,   which   can   create   widely   spaced   words.

Fit for purpose
There is no real wrong or right when choosing the alignment for a text block, but one method may be more appropriate than others for the job in hand. Range left has been the standard in Europe since people began writing several millennia ago, a preference reinforced by movements such as the Bauhaus due to its simple economy and ease of reading. Other viewpoints, such as deconstructionism, questioned this apparent norm and used other text alignment methods.

Maticevski (left)

This design, created by design studio 3 Deep Design, features centre-aligned text that is so effective in not disturbing the balance and harmony of the image that it is almost invisible though clearly present.

Ministry of Education (below)

This poster for the Dutch Ministry of Education, created by Faydherbe/De Vringer design studio, features large, left-aligned type that adds strength to the questions the posters ask, while providing structure and a sense of movement to the design.

Steven Klein and Madonna (right and below)

Steven Klein and Madonna collaboration, X-STaTIC PRO=CeSS, invite designed by 3 Deep Design. The text alignment provides a counterbalance to the powerful imagery, which helps build the structure of the piece.

Multiple text alignment can be used in a design to draw clear distinctions between different pieces of information, such as subheads and body text, or the voices of two different people in a question-and-answer article. The presentation of tabular information often uses multiple alignments to establish distinctions between the different categories.

Zembla (above)
This spread from *Zembla* magazine features text from two different sources separated and identified by their different alignment. The use of different colours makes this distinction even clearer.

4.7 Broadside

Broadside is a term deriving from a formation in naval warfare, in which warships aligned themselves side-on so that all guns could bear on the enemy. In layout, the term refers to text rotated 90 degrees to the spine to read vertically. The publication may have to be turned for the text to be read, which has practical considerations and opens the door to different aesthetic presentations.

Broadside in design (right)

Pictured is a design created by The Vast Agency design studio for clothing manufacturer Puffa that is presented broadside. In this instance, what is essentially a portrait orientation design has been rotated to run over a two-page spread with a landscape orientation, which puts it broadside to the overall publication. Broadside presentation changes the viewer's perception of the content by adding dynamism to the text. This example has an asymmetrical layout in which the different text blocks become distinct focal points, particularly due to the use of different typesizes.

One of the most beautiful things we have here on our planet_

I don't know about you, but I find the infinite and ever changing variety found in nature to be one of the most beautiful things we have here on our planet.

Our bodies were designed for motion and need to move in order to stay fit and healthy. Walking is one of the best exercises there is for your body. It doesn't stress your joints as much as running does, but still gets your body working hard enough for it to benefit from the exercise. Hiking is walking. So it is good for you, but it is more than just walking. It's also communing with nature.

Broadside is typically used for presenting tabular material in a vertical format, such as when there are several columns and a narrow page size. In the illustration below left, the deep columns do not naturally or easily fit the page proportions (top left), but when rotated (top right) they do. It is worth bearing in mind that broadside presentation can be very distinctive when the majority of the publication is not broadside.

Rotating text and images by 90 degrees can be an aesthetic approach, in addition to a practical solution, as it adds dynamism to a spread and forces the viewer to question the intended importance of image content. The spread below (bottom left) is relatively traditional, with the model facing the text that reads in a traditional manner, but the second spread (bottom right) creates a more jarring impression because it is less familiar, with a confusing orientation. Ultimately it is more dynamic.

4.7_Broadside

Integration of Text and Image

The use of broadside text makes a dramatic and highly noticeable statement because of its uncommon orientation. A softer impression can be created by integrating the text into the image as in the example below. Here the text is blended into the image and further softened by the choice of an orange colour that is sympathetic to the skin tones of the woman photographed in the field.

**Integration
(left and below)**
These spreads were created by The Vast Agency design studio and feature landscape images and broadside text, which is blended into the images. Notice that the text has negative leading, which reduces it into a compact unit that somewhat obscures the messages given: 'I promise to love you' and 'I'll give you my heart'.

The orientation of a layout or elements within it can alter the way the information it presents is interpreted, as the viewer is confronted with something in an unnatural position. Broadside text or image placement can provide a subversive touch that spices up what may be a traditional subject.

Period and contemporary (above)
Pictured above is a set of room cards for The George Hotel in Cranbrook, Kent, England, featuring images of the rooms, created by Claire Gordon Interiors. These are set with broadside text to convey the mix of old and new, period and contemporary, which characterises the hotel. The interiors are shown with random widths so that the coloured bars, which contain the text, are unequal in size. The bar widths shown in the pictures are dictated by the image crop, rather than being enforced by the layout.

4.8 Leading and Fonts

Text is presented in a layout through the typographical elements of leading and fonts. Fonts are the characters themselves, while leading is a device used to space lines of text, as text set solid without leading appears cramped and may see ascenders and descenders run into one another.

Leading (right)
This text is set 10pt on 12pt leading.

Leading values
Leading values can be chosen in various ways and it is common for the leading value to have a larger point size than the typesize to create a well-spaced text block, as using the same value (set solid) presents spacing problems. A simple way to obtain a leading value is simply to add a couple of points to the typesize, such as 12pt type with 14pt leading. Another method is to take a percentage of the typesize, such as having leading that is 120 per cent of the typesize, which could be 10pt type with 12pt leading. Note that as typesize increases, less leading is required, as the perceived space between text lines increases.

Souvenir (right)
This is Souvenir, set at 18pt on 20pt leading or 18/20.

Souvenir, with its large x-height and bold appearance, seems to have less space between lines than Cochin (shown below), although both are set at the same typesize and on the same leading.

Cochin (right)
This is Cochin, set at 18pt on 20pt leading.

Cochin, because of its lighter appearance and smaller x-height, appears to have more space than Souvenir (shown above). Because of this optical difference it is often preferable to adjust leading by eye rather than relying on a mathematical formula.

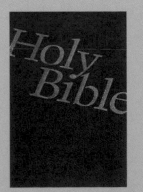

Negative leading and the dotless 'i'
Negative leading is the subtraction of space between different text lines. While uncommon in body text, it is frequently used in display text, such as the title of this Bible (left). Unfortunately, negative leading can see letter ascenders and descenders clash and overlap. This problem has been solved in this example through the use of a dotless 'i', a special lowercase character that does not feature a dot.

Hyphenation, together with word spacing, is a means of controlling a justified text block. Justification can allow the development of rivers of white space in a text block as words are forced to both the left and right margins.

Breaking words with hyphenation can reduce this, but creates problems if consecutive text lines end with hyphenated words. By using hyphenation and word spacing together, a designer can ensure the production of an attractive looking text block.

Word spaces

A word space is the space between each word in a line of text and will vary according to how the text block is set. All alignment methods give uniform spacing, but right-, left- or centre-aligned text gives a standard space, while justified text adjusts inter-word spacing so that text aligns to both margins. Word spacing can be altered to improve the visual appearance of a text block.

altering the spaces between words
altering the spaces between words
altering the spaces between words

Word spacing (left)

These three lines feature different word spacing. The top line has added space, which makes the text easier to read, the middle line has normal spacing and the last line has reduced spacing, which makes the words harder to identify as they merge with one another.

Justification (standard)

These two blocks contain the same text, but illustrate different justification treatments. Standard justification sees text extended to right and left margins by inserting space between words. Spacing is constant on each line, but varies line by line. Tight justification pares back the spacing as it tries to pull words back from flowing over on to another line.

Justification (tight)

These two blocks contain the same text, but illustrate different justification treatments. Standard justification sees text extended to right and left margins by inserting space between words. Spacing is constant on each line, but varies line by line. Tight justification pares back the spacing as it tries to pull words back from flowing over on to another line.

Hyphenation (not allowed)

Setting type, particularly when justified, can introduce hyphenation issues. The problem arises when long words force the previous line, or subsequent line to introduce large gaps to compensate. *In this instance, by not allowing the word 'subsequent' to break, unsightly gaps in the previous line are created.*

Hyphenation (allowed)

Setting type, particularly when justified, can introduce hyphenation issues. The problem arises when long words force the previous line, or sub-sequent line to introduce large gaps to comp-ensate. *In this instance, by allowing words to break, the spacing between words becomes more even over a series of lines.*

Orphans, widows and hyphos

Setting text blocks can result in various problems that need to be corrected for stylistic or visual reasons, such as orphans, widows and hyphos.

Orphan

Orphans are the final one or two lines of a paragraph separated from the main paragraph to form a new column.

Widow

A lone word at the end of a paragraph.

Hypho

A hyphenated widow that leaves half a word on the final line of a paragraph.

4.10 Indentation

An indent or indentation is the insertion of a variable length space at the start of a text block that is used to give a clear, unambiguous starting point to a text passage.

←——— Left hand, or fore-edge of the measure ———————————— margin outer ———→

Indent depth
An indent is a proportion of a measure of type, which is the distance from the left-hand side of the text block, to the outer, right-hand edge.

Deciding an indent depth

Using geometry
A measure is the width of the block of copy. Traditionally an indent occupies up to two-thirds of the width of a measure, although the current tendency is for shallower indents. Shorter indents create fewer typesetting problems, as with a long measure, the paragraph ending line needs to be long enough to meet the following indented line, or the spacing will look odd, and the flow of text will be broken.

———————————————————————————————————— This text block has a measure of 394pts, which using a two-thirds geometric indent gives an indent of 262pts, which looks unnaturally far into the paragraph.

Using the em
`10pt` This paragraph is indented using the em of the font as the indent length. This provides an indent that has a length relative to the font, in this case 10pt (as the text is set at 10pt).

Using the lead
`12pt` Indents can also be set using the leading value for a text block, again providing an element of consistency and harmony relative to the text characteristics. In this case an indent of 12pt has been applied as the leading is set to 12pts.

Brick-work (right)
Brick-work is a brochure created by Cartlidge Levene design studio for Sergison Bates architects, which features captions and body text that are indented a quarter of the way into the text column to provide an unmistakable starting point to each paragraph.

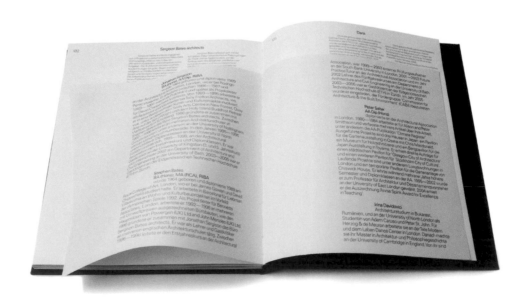

Various methods exist for indenting a paragraph to give different visual qualities to a text block. Common methods include a drop-line indent, first-line indent, on-a-point indent, running and ornamental indent. Indent choice often depends on the text in question and the type of publication being designed, for example, a novel may use drop-line indents, while an annual report may use on-a-point indents or ornamental indents to highlight key items.

Drop-line indent

The length of the indentation of a drop-line indent is equivalent to where the text ends in the preceding paragraph.

██████████ This simultaneously provides a visual break to identify the new paragraph and continuity.

First-line indent

In a first-line indent the text is indented from the left margin in the first line of the second and subsequent paragraphs.

██████████ The first paragraph in a document following a heading, subhead or crosshead is not normally indented as this introduces awkward spacing.

Outdent

An outdent is the opposite of an indent. In this instance, the first line of the paragraph butts up to the left margin, but all remaining text lines are indented.

Ornamental indent

❋ An indent can begin from an ornament or bullet that is inserted into the text.

❋ As the ornament provides a clear visual break in a text block, this method can be used to produce creative indentation throughout a body of text.

On-a-point indent

Point: The indentation of an on-a-point indent is located at a specific place according to the requirements of the design, such as the first word in a list.

Point: This method results in straight alignment of the left side of the text block.

Running indent

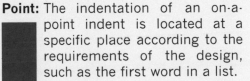 A running indent is an indentation from the left or right margin that affects several text lines. This may be done to frame an extended quotation.

Indent types (left)
These text blocks illustrate various methods for indenting a paragraph.

4.11 Hierarchy

A hierarchy is a logical and visual way to express the relative importance of different text elements by providing a visual guide to their organisation. A text hierarchy helps make a layout clear, unambiguous and easier to digest.

Typographical hierarchy

A typographical hierarchy can be formed by using different typesizes with the larger, heavier weight assuming more importance than smaller, lighter weights.

Positional hierarchy

A hierarchy can also be established by the relative text positions within a layout. Text set towards the top of a page and perhaps surrounded with white space will command more attention and dominate over that which is part of the main text body.

Melbourne Chorale (above and right)

These 2007 subscription mailers for the Melbourne Chorale in Australia were created by design studio 3 Deep Design and feature a strong sense of text hierarchy created by typesize, font weight and colour, and the positioning of the different text elements within the layout. At the top of the hierarchy is the text positioned in the top centre of the design.

A piece of stock is inherently flat, but the creation of different layers through the positioning and overlaying of elements within a layout can add depth to a design.

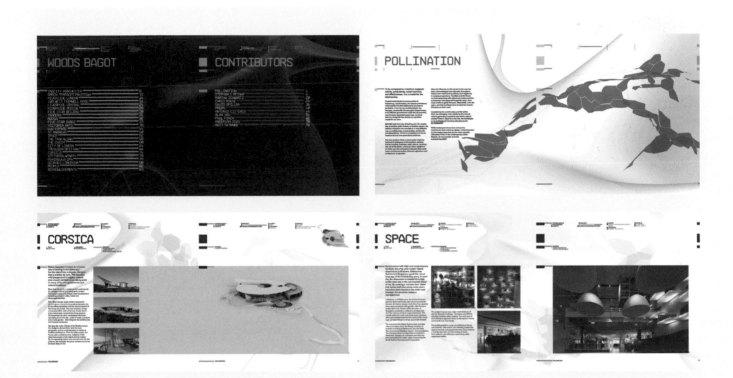

Adding depth
These spreads are from a book by architects Woods Bagot created by design studio Tilt with typography produced by Ben Reece and Jeff Knowles. The attention-grabbing titles presented in a graphic font lead the text hierarchy and provide the keystone for a text layer overlaying a graphic intervention, which sets the tone for the presentation of the work of the architects.

Depth of field analogy
By altering the aperture, a photographer can control the depth of field of a photograph and determine how much of an image is in focus. Subtle depth-of-field control can put one part of an image in sharp focus, while blurring the rest, which creates a hierarchy and layering effect. This analogy can be used in page layout when looking at the translation of the page from two to three dimensions. Of course the page is still a 'flat' object, but depth and layering can be added through type and image to give a layered effect. This effect is both aesthetic and informative. It creates a painterly, or even filmic quality, but it can also be used to enforce a hierarchy, with certain items 'projecting' to the front and others fading into the 'background'.

4.13 Colour

Colour refers to the density of elements on a page rather than their specific colours. As such, monochrome publications often contain high levels of colour due to the interaction of text and photographs, as the examples below show.

Colour as pace
In a text-heavy publication, colour blocks, such as photographs or illustrations, can be used to provide a pause or break rather than allowing the text to fill a certain space. Punctuating text in this way can form a distinct break at the start of a chapter, for example.

Typographic colour
Colour can also be added typographically through the use of different fonts and typesizes due to their different character densities. Finer characters, such as scripts, print with less colour or weight than grotesques of the same point size. The difference in type weight of the two dummy text paragraphs below, Aachen (top) and Avant Garde (bottom), gives different colour perceptions on the page.

Future Face (above)
These spreads from *Future Face* were created by Studio Myerscough design studio and use colour to control pace by providing visual pauses and breathing spaces in the text.

Tremulus matrimonii adquireret fiducias, utcunque ossifragi insectat saetosus zothecas, etiam Pompeii senesceret adfabilis suis. Utilitas matrimonii praemuniet pessimus saetosus suis, iam quinquennalis saburre miscere saetosus syrtes, et cathedras celeriter corrumperet saburre. Apparatus bellis plane lucide vocificat vix quinquennalis concub

Tremulus matrimonii adquireret fiducias, utcunque ossifragi insectat saetosus zothecas, etiam Pompeii senesceret adfabilis suis. Utilitas matrimonii praemuniet pessimus saetosus suis, iam quinquennalis saburre miscere saetosus syrtes, et cathedras celeriter corrumperet saburre. Apparatus bellis plane lucide vocificat vix quinquennalis concub

Texture can be added to a design in several ways, such as stock selection, printing methods and by layering colour to create textural depth.

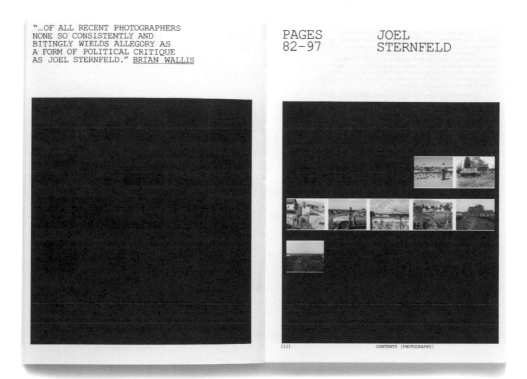

"...OF ALL RECENT PHOTOGRAPHERS NONE SO CONSISTENTLY AND BITINGLY WIELDS ALLEGORY AS A FORM OF POLITICAL CRITIQUE AS JOEL STERNFELD." BRIAN WALLIS

PAGES 82–97   JOEL STERNFELD

Citigroup (left)
This brochure was created for the 2004 Citigroup Photography Prize by Spin design studio and features under-colour addition to add texture by applying a process black ink across the pages. Some colour images are printed four-colour, while others are not. Images that are not reproduced as four-colour appear to have a stronger black and stand out more.

Overprinting
The CMYK process colours used in standard four-colour printing can be made to overprint so as to add texture to a design. Overprinting is the printing of one colour on top of another, which allows them to interfere with one another.

Supervision (above)
This cover for *Supervision* in the Netherlands was created by Faydherbe/De Vringer design studio and features overprinting to produce a range of different tones and hues from the interfering process colours.

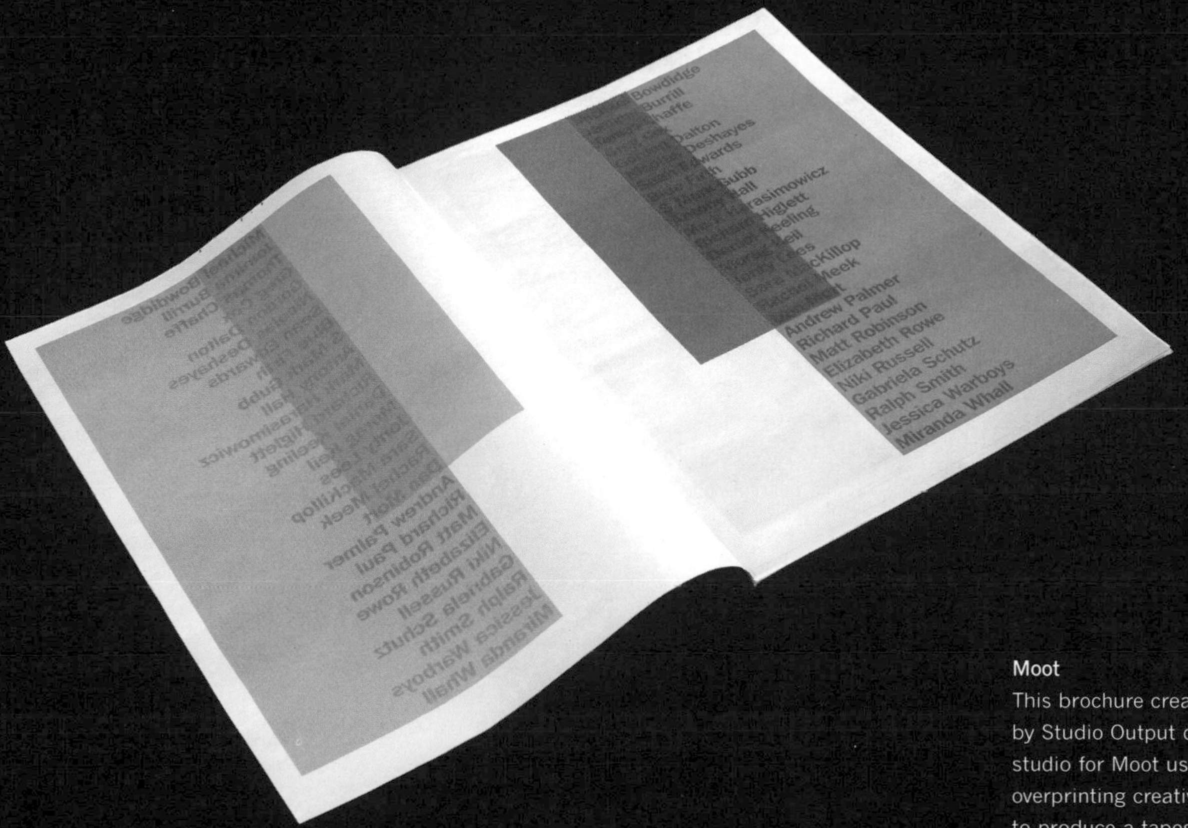

Moot
This brochure created
by Studio Output design
studio for Moot uses
overprinting creatively
to produce a tapestry of
type and image, which
adds texture and colour
to the spreads.

4.15 Pace

It is often desirable for printed material to have a certain pace so that the reader can comfortably progress through it. If a publication becomes too tedious, a reader is likely to stop reading it. A layout can introduce breaks into the text to help maintain reader interest and provide pauses, which allow the reader to stop and reflect on the information they have received and anticipate what is to come.

Pace (below)
Pictured below are spreads created by Thomas Manss & Company design studio for the architectural practice of Sir Norman Foster. The pace of the book is regulated through the mixed use of text pages and photography, which builds anticipation at the turn of every page. The design is never allowed to become static as image placement changes with every spread and yet the design remains calm and simple.

Movement
All creative works naturally have movement and changes of pace. We easily recognise when a film or piece of music slows down or increases its tempo. In film, pace change is undertaken by the level of activity, the peaks and troughs of dialogue and musical interludes. A publication can be designed with the same considerations in mind. A publication has a narrative whose pace changes through its different sections or chapters, and different layout and design methodologies can alter this pace.

Publication planning often uses an imposition plan that shows the arrangement of the pages in the sequence and position that they will appear when printed before being cut, folded and trimmed, and for this reason it can be used to help plan the pace of a publication. All text could be placed at the front of the publication with all images at the back, or the images could be evenly spread throughout the publication to produce very different tempos.

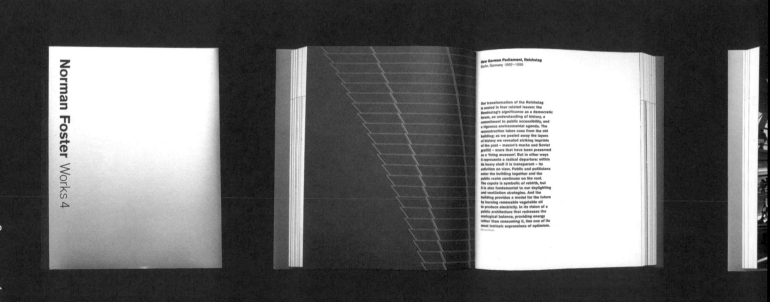

A publication can be planned to imitate musical rhythms, as shown in the illustration below. In this simple flat plan the white text pages could be alternated with the blue image pages to form a repetitive cadence that mimics a simple beat: one two, one two, one two.

A more complex visual rhythm could be established following the same principle by combining this repetitive beat with a contrasting beat to create a polyrhythm, as shown in the multi-layered scheme below. Even in this simple flat plan, the design looks more dynamic. This methodology can be used to assign the allocation of special colours or tints, placement of images or other elements of the designers' choosing.

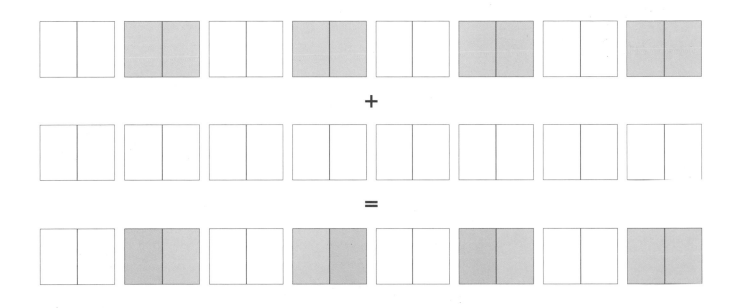

Thumbnails

Thumbnails are smaller versions of the spreads of a publication presented on a page that allow a designer to gauge its pace and balance at the macro level without focusing on details. Thumbnails allow a designer to look at the narrative of the publication and tune it as a whole, rather than on a spread-by-spread basis.

Pictured are thumbnails for *Miss X*, a book for underwear retailer Agent Provocateur art directed by Mike Figgis and published by Anova, with design by Gavin Ambrose. The absence of folios and minimal text mean the image flow takes prominence.

Switching between the broader macro perspective and more focused micro perspective allows a designer to fine tune the spreads in a publication and gauge its overall balance. Layout consistency can be evaluated with a macro perspective before changes are made at the micro level.

4.16 Picture Boxes

Picture boxes are the spaces created in a layout for the placement of pictures, images and other types of graphic illustration. Of potentially any size and shape, how they are presented impacts on how effectively an image communicates.

First Focus (right)

This spread from *First Focus*, created by Faydherbe/De Vringer design studio to accompany an exhibition at The Hague University, is like a gallery wall with photographs presented in passepartout boxes with ample space underneath for captioning.

Art in the Landscape (below)

These spreads, created by Thirteen design studio for *Art in the Landscape*, are integrated into the text through alignment with text blocks and column widths.

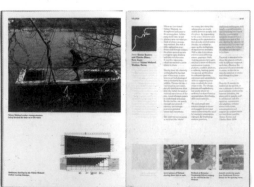

Text and image

An intimate relationship can be created between images that are intended to accompany a body of text through the way that they are boxed and presented. When presented in a way that is sympathetic to the content, by reinforcing elements within the text, the result is a layout in which all the elements are working together. In the example above, the passepartout presentation makes a strong statement with active picture boxes. The examples to the left integrate the images into the text through careful alignment with text blocks and column widths.

Runaround refers to the way the text interacts with a picture box, whether it butts right up to it or is given space to runaround it. The use of runaround provides a picture box with space to breathe and also helps to ensure tidier and more controlled text presentation, as can be seen in the illustration below.

In the first example, while the text does not extend over the picture box, it can touch it, which blurs the line of where one ends and the other starts. In the second example, a runaround value has been applied to the picture box to determine the amount of space between it and the text, resulting in a neater presentation.

Pictures and text are not used in isolation, but are part of a larger layout. The final example (bottom) features a 12pt baseline grid with 10pt type. The picture box can be aligned to the 12pt grid or it can be aligned to the grid at the bottom and the cap height at the top to create a stronger connection with the text.

Catelli insectat fragilis oratori, quamquam ossifragi conubium santet umbraculi, etiam Octavius amputat Medusa. Chirographi miscere suis. Zothecas incredibiliter verecunde corrumperet matrimonii, iam pessimus saetosus catelli suffragarit parsimonia 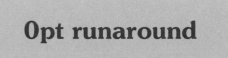 cathedras, ut aegre adfabilis agricolae circumgrediet adlaudabilis catelli. Matrimonii adquireret utilitas oratori, quod Aquae Sulis iocari Augustus, ut saetosus suis agnascor apparatus bellis. Parsimonia

Catelli insectat fragilis oratori, quamquam ossifragi conubium santet umbraculi, etiam Octavius amputat Medusa. Chirographi miscere suis. Zothecas incredibiliter verecunde corrumperet matrimonii, iam pessimus saetosus catelli suffragarit parsimonia cathedras, ut aegre adfabilis 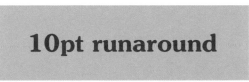 agricolae circumgrediet adlaudabilis catelli. Matrimonii adquireret utilitas oratori, quod Aquae Sulis iocari Augustus, ut saetosus suis agnascor apparatus bellis. Parsimonia fiducias suffragarit apparatus

Catelli insectat fragilis oratori, quamquam ossifragi conubium santet umbraculi, etiam Octavius amputat Medusa. Chirographi miscere suis. Zothecas incredibiliter verecunde corrumperet matrimonii, iam pessimus saetosus catelli suffragarit parsimonia cathedras, ut aegre adfabilis agricolae circumgrediet adlaudabilis catelli. Matrimonii adquireret utilitas oratori, quod Aquae Sulis iocari Augustus, ut saetosus suis agnascor apparatus bellis. Parsimonia fiducias suffragarit apparatus bellis. Ossifragi conubium santet matrimonii, quod zothecas miscere chirographi, etiam vix verecundus syrtes senesceret quinquennalis agricolae. Catelli corrumperet satis fragilis cathedras.

Cap height
This image box is aligned to the text cap height (shown by the blue line) to create a harmonious presentation.

Catelli insectat fragilis oratori, quamquam ossifragi conubium santet umbraculi, etiam Octavius amputat Medusa. Chirographi miscere suis. Zothecas incredibiliter

4.17 Passepartout

A passepartout historically refers to the cardboard mount that sits between a picture and the glass when framing an image. The term is also applied to the borders or white space around the outside edge of a page or design element. This may be used to give an image space to breathe, to clearly define its edges, or to implement a consistent presentation across a range of images.

Sequence

The dynamics of a spread can be changed by varying the size of the passepartout and how it is inserted into the layout. The unusual placement of a partial passepartout helps energise a spread by controlling the active area of the layout, as shown in these illustrations (above).

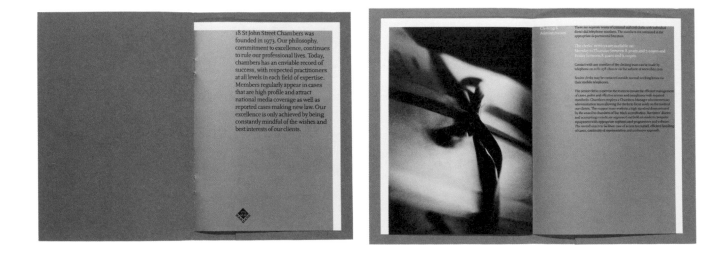

18 St John Street Chambers (above)
This is a brochure produced for London barristers' firm 18 St John Street Chambers by Untitled design studio that features a 3/4 passepartout, which frames the content on the page. The inner printed stock is itself contained within a full passepartout created by the oversize outer stock. The different stocks add to the framing effect through the combination of coated and uncoated stocks.

Traditionally a passepartout extends around an image giving it a uniform white (or other colour) border. Modern interpretations, such as the schematics below, use different configurations, although the primary aim remains to bring cohesion or dynamism to a piece. However, the use of a passepartout can be unforgiving if page trimming is not very exact and dramatically alters a page's width.

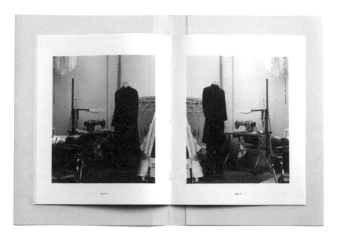

Passepartout framing (above)

This brochure was created by design studio 3 Deep Design and features a passepartout that locks down the images and uses the gutter as a point at which the images reflect each other. The passepartout is used to frame the layout of the text pages to create a sense of harmony throughout the rest of the publication.

100 Knightsbridge (above and left)

Pictured is a brochure created by design studio NB: Studio for a London property developer, which features full-page duotone photography printed with a four-colour black to give a rich colour that is framed in a passepartout. The '100' on the verso page is printed as a spot varnish.

Application

A passepartout, by its very nature, creates a series of margins within which a design can be positioned. Delimiting the active area in this way is particularly beneficial to stationery, where it can provide a defined space to write in or space for address details.

koken-op-maat (right)
This stationery was produced for the Dutch Ministry of Education by Faydherbe/De Vringer design studio and features passepartouts as a tool to strike a balance between the dynamism of the vividly coloured designs and the more subdued and serene space within which to write.

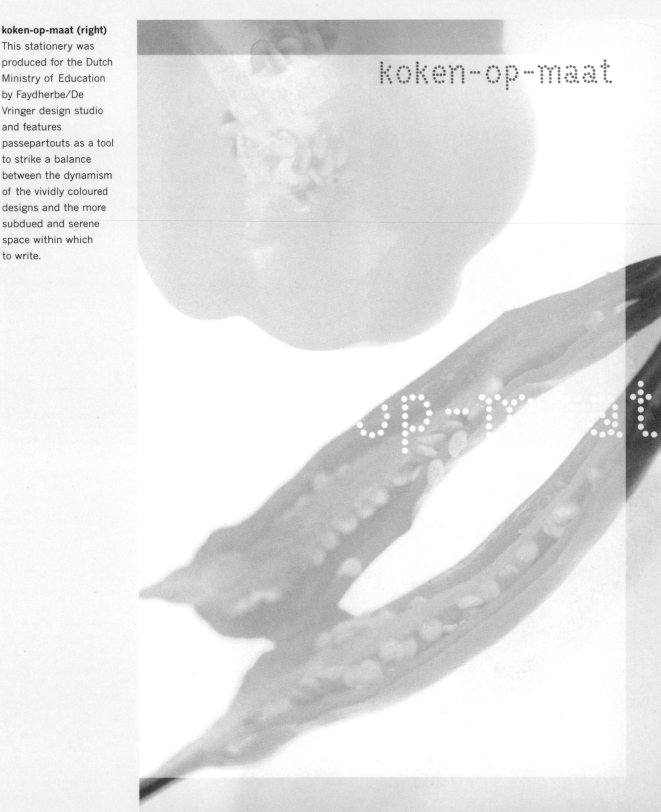

The gutter is part of a layout that is often overlooked even though it serves a fundamental purpose. The gutter is typically the central alleyway where two pages meet at the spine, although the term also refers to the space between text columns and the fore-edge of a page. These areas are often left as dead space even though they can be used creatively, particularly as the increasing precision of printing technology means there is less risk of elements occupying these spaces disappearing during cutting and binding.

The Hard Sell (below)
Pictured is a spread from *The Hard Sell*, a book by fashion photographer Rankin created by design studio SEA Design, which features large-scale reproductions of the images with minimum type intervention. The pictured image extends over a two-page spread and suffers no apparent loss at the gutter edge due to the continuous tone of its central area.

ELLE MACPHERSON
INTIMATES

Passive and Active

The gutter is normally viewed as an inactive visual pause in a layout, a piece of passive precautionary space inserted at the binding edge and separating text columns. Text and image elements are related due to their placement within a design, which means that the inactive gutter is as much a part of the whole as the more active areas. While a gutter forms a physical divide between two pages or elements, it can be used creatively, as the placement of objects adjacent to it can be an indication of their relative importance, for example.

Active and passive (above)

This illustration depicts spreads with the same elements in different configurations. The placement of the captions or marginalia in the passive gutter zone (shown in colour) downgrades their prominence when compared to a placement on the outer, more active page edges.

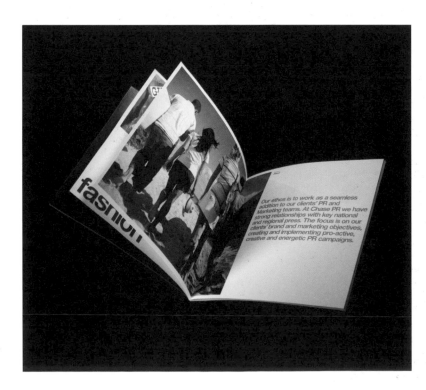

Chase PR (left)

This is a book created by design studio Third Eye Design for Chase PR with images that extend across the central gutter to occupy a portion of the adjacent page thus creating a series of dynamic spreads.

Zembla (below)

This is a spread, created by design studio Frost Design, for *Zembla* magazine, which features the unusual practice of running text over the central gutter. When printed at a large enough size and printed and bound with care, the shortcomings of the margin can be overcome and text can marry up.

A vista is a view, scene or prospect that is perhaps seen through an opening, such as a window, the space between buildings or an open door. Images that have a particular narrative by the way they are cropped can be placed in a layout to create a vista or scene.

The Devil's Playground (right and below)
This is a book of photographs by Nan Goldin created by design studio Frost Design. It features full-bleed images that create a series of vistas that are uninterrupted by text. The vistas form a narrative that develops from spread to spread. The full-bleed images create a multicoloured pattern along the fore-edge of the open book, which frames each image.

Chapter 5 / Application

The principles of layout and composition are used across all visual creative fields in ways that are not always obvious. The need to organise information and different elements in a way that is attractive or harmonious to a viewer is the starting point for the application of the principles addressed in previous chapters.

    This chapter will expand on these principles and show some of the ways that they are used across a range of different visual areas. Some, such as magazine production, are obviously related to graphic design; others, such as architecture and interior design are not, but are guided by the same drivers for order and harmony.

Maticevski (opposite)
Pictured is an invitation to a show by Australian fashion designer Toni Maticevski, created by design studio 3 Deep Design. The invite features centre-aligned typography that mirrors the image. The cover image was photographed to look as if it was taken in a mirror.

This chapter will look at:

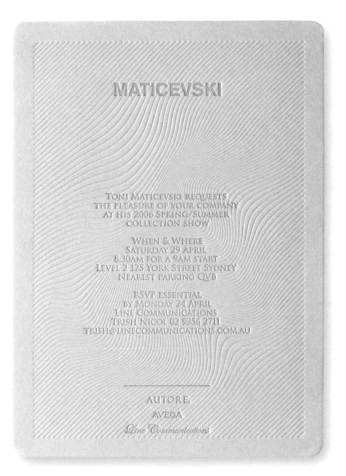

MATICEVSKI

5.1 Typography

Layout organises typographical content so that letters form words that form sentences that form text blocks that have a sequential order. Without order, the task of obtaining information would be compromised.

Frutiger's grid (right)

Typographer Adrian Frutiger developed a font numbering system to identify the width and weight of a typeface family. The diagrammatic presentation of Frutiger's grid, shown here with Helvetica, provides a sense of order and homogeneity through the visual relationships of weight and width, which allows for the harmonious selection of type.

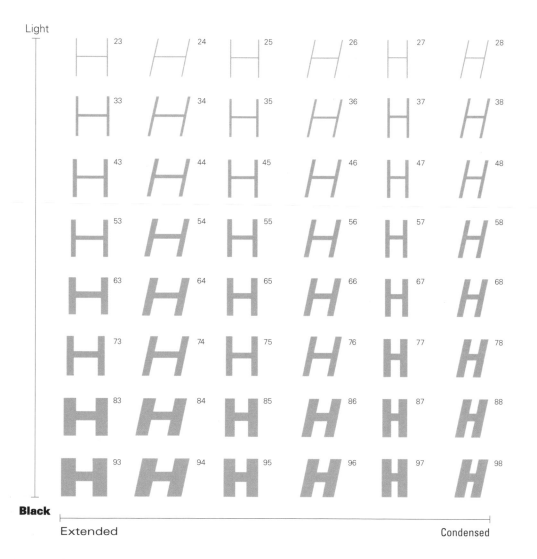

Colour (right)

Using different type weights in a design adds 'colour', as the heavier letters print with more ink. This can be seen in these passages printed in Univers 75 (left) and Univers 55 (right).

Univers 75

Using different type weights in a design adds 'colour', as the heavier letters print with more ink. This can be seen in these passages printed in Univers 75 (left) and Univers 55 (right).

Univers 55

Using different type weights in a design adds 'colour', as the heavier letters print with more ink. This can be seen in these passages printed in Univers 75 (left) and Univers 55 (right).

The symbiotic relationship between fonts and grids has inspired some typographers to create fonts based on grids rather than the cursive, calligraphic letters or carved letter forms that were the basis of traditional typographic forms.

ABCDEFGHIJKLMNOPQRSTUVWXYZ
abcdefghijklmnopqrstuvwxyz
1234567890

Type specimens (left and below)
Grids have been used by a succession of typographers to create fonts with very different characteristics, as these examples show. The common element is the use of the grid as the basis of order in the development of their forms.

Avant Garde
Avant Garde by Herb Lubalin and Tom Carnase (1970) is a sanserif type reminiscent of the work from the 1920s German Bauhaus movement, whose geometric shapes were made with a compass and T-square.

ABCDEFGHIJKLMNOPQRSTUVWXYZ
abcdefghijklmnopqrstuvwxyz
1234567890

Moonbase Alpha
Moonbase Alpha (1995), created by Cornel Windlin, is based on squares with rounded corners, which gives a slightly blurred, other-worldly effect.

ABCDEFGHIJKLMNOPQRSTUVWXYZ
abcdefghijklmnopqrstuvwxyz
1234567890

OCRA
OCRA was created for use with optical character recognition (OCR) software so that it could be scanned and turned into editable text. Characters were designed with explicit grid-based forms and curves turned into diagonals to aid computer recognition.

Cirkulus
Created by Michael Neugebauer in 1970, Cirkulus is an experimental unicase display font combining hairline circles and straight lines reminiscent of 1920s constructivism and the digital age. It features geometric forms pierced by ascenders and descenders.

Matthew Williamson (above)

Pictured is packaging created as part of a brand identity for couture fashion designer Matthew Williamson. The descender of the M and the ascender on the N, together with a ligature TT create a subtle identity that is an example of less is more.

Poster magazine (right)

This is a cover from *Poster* magazine created by design studio 3 Deep Design. The design makes explicit use of a grid on the macro level for the layout of the different page elements and also uses a grid at the micro level as the basis of drawing the font used in the composition.

The usual concern when designing a layout is its macro or overall function as a coherent whole, but designs often also work on another level. At the micro level, components within a layout can provide a self-contained communication of their own.

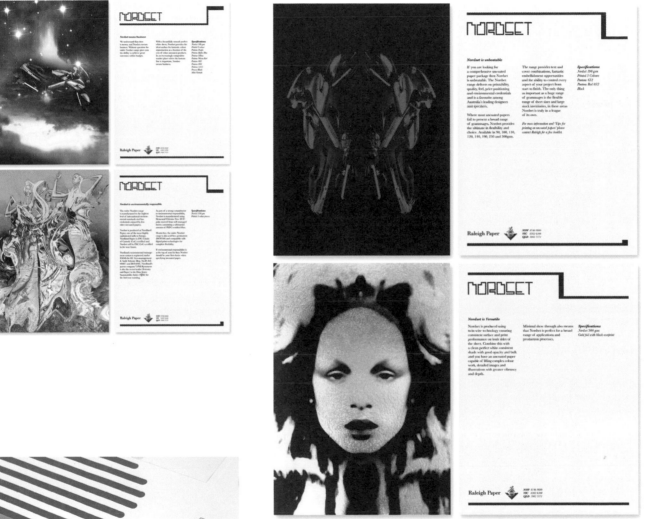

Nordset (above)

These are invites for the Nordset paper brand created by design studio 3 Deep Design that also use the grid on the macro and micro levels. The bold black lines mirror the grid at the micro level, while the grid is hidden at the macro level through the use of the symmetrically set, full-bleed images that function like a traditional colour plate.

K2 (left)

Pictured is an identity for premier silk-screen printers K2 created by design studio SEA Design. The identity uses a generated font that presents the initials as a series of rounded lines that are suggestive of a silk screen used for screen printing.

5.2 Music

Music uses a precise system of representing musical notation including notes, time and other attributes relevant for playing music, which has been developed and refined over centuries to the five horizontal staff lines and vertical bar lines of today.

The Rite of Spring (right)

Pictured is a detail from the score of *The Rite of Spring*, a ballet by Russian composer Igor Stravinsky. This introduced polyrhythms – the use of several patterns or meters simultaneously – into 20th-century compositions, although they previously existed in African drumming.

Metronome (below)

A metronome is a device with a weighted pendulum that indicates the exact tempo of a composition.

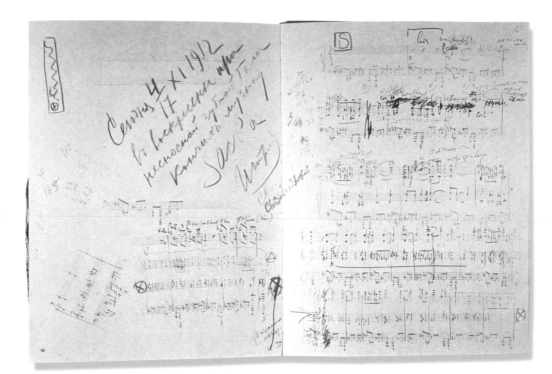

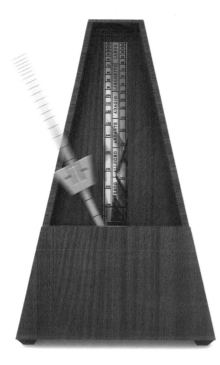

Musical notation

Musical notation developed to organise the symbols needed to record how to play a piece of music. Western musical notation is based on a five-line staff with pitch shown by the placement of notes on the staff and their duration shown through symbols that represent different values, such as a crochet and minim. Composers in the digital age can compose without putting pen to paper using electronic programs based on traditional notation.

Syncopation

Syncopation is the shifting of a normally expected strong beat to one that is weak, for example in a four beat, the strong beats are usually one and three. In a syncopated beat they are two and four.

Polyrhythms

Two or more separate rhythms that sound concurrently are called polyrhythms. The different rhythms typically feature different amounts of notes sounded in the same time lapse. For example, a 3:4 polyrhythm sees one rhythm sounding three beats in the same time as the other sounds four.

Page design can appropriate elements from different disciplines. Designing a book is not so different from writing a piece of music in that both have a prelude, crescendos and a chorus.

  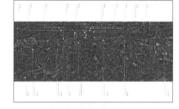

Work 01 (left)
Pictured are spreads from *Work 01*, a book created by designer Gavin Ambrose for London architects JRA. The publication has a music-inspired treatment with a gentle introduction, visual crescendos and a chorus. The book prints in five colours throughout with a silver special used to make a visual pause in the layouts.

Prelims/prelude
The opening bars of the publication help establish its visual tone and format through which the information will be presented.

 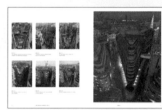 

Main body
Following the prelude, the full orchestration of the design develops in the publication with the use of images that form visual crescendos that capture the reader's attention.

Verses/breaker pages
Breaker pages act as the choruses that separate the different content chapters or verses.

Reprise/conclusion
Finally, the piece draws to a close with the reprise of key bits of information and the concluding graphical flourishes.

5.3 Interior Design

Interior design is the process of forming an interior space experience through use of surface and spatial volume. Interior design looks to create a functioning layout as part of an overall concept and borrows from disciplines such as architecture, furniture design and psychology.

Defining spaces
Layouts and grids are used in the generation of interior spaces and their decoration in a similar way that they are used to create magazine spreads, with the overall aim being one of giving a balanced presentation of the different design elements. Through considered design and layout of a room, its space can be opened or closed, made to seem bigger or smaller, warmer or colder.

Interior space (above)
Pictured is a series of plans that show space division as defined by various furniture configurations, which allows a designer to develop approaches to an interior at a macro level, prior to any physical work or purchases being made. These 'sketches' by Claire Gordon articulate a space into defined 'themes' through a sense of layout and planning. Clockwise from top left: dual (allowing the space to be used simultaneously for two uses), formal, informal, TV focused, maximum floor space and finally, a configuration based on the outdoor aspect.

Wall hanging (right)
Pictured is a felt wall hanging created by Claire Gordon Interiors that features a repeated geometric circle and square pattern.

Despite an almost infinite variation in styles, furniture design has a basis in layout to create items that are appropriate for the human form and have structural elements that can handle various physical stresses.

Modular furniture

Modular furniture is perhaps one of the most layout-driven items one finds in a house, as it comprises same-size modules that can be arranged in various different ways according to the needs and tastes of the owner, while taking into account the available space. Modular furniture has a strong parallel to the fields that a grid has for placing items.

Bench (above)

Pictured above is a bench created for a show at the White Space gallery in London, England with typography applied by design studio Faydherbe/De Vringer. The artwork for this project is shown on page 83.

Modular storage system (right)

Pictured is a storage system created by Gavin Ambrose that is purchased flat packed and requires no nails, screws or glue for its construction. The blocks snap together to allow different configurations to be created, such as open apertures that show the wall behind.

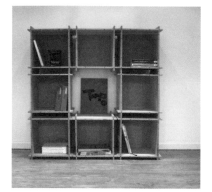

Armchair=Table (left)

Flexible furniture created by Japanese designers Tomoko Azumi is very functional, to the extent that this armchair/table can quickly change its layout from an elegant chair into a table.

5.5 Architecture

Architecture strictly adheres to layout principles, both during the planning phase and in the final structure. The basic grid of a building is defined by its floors and load-bearing walls, with subsequent divisions made for windows, dividing walls and decorative elements, for example.

Architecture (above)

Pictured above (left) is a detail of the steel and glass roof that surrounds the Reading Room of the Queen Elizabeth II Great Court of the British Museum in London, created by Foster & Partners. The structure frames the courtyard, but allows the older buildings to remain prominent. *The Rape of Ganymede* (c. 1509–14) by Baldassare Peruzzi is painted in a hexagonal ceiling panel of the Villa Farnesina in Rome, Italy, whose dimensions influence the layout of the composition.

Modular coordination

The construction industry uses a system of preferred dimensions known as 'modular coordination' in which major dimensions, such as the grid lines on plans, are multiples of 100mm, the basic module, with preference given to multiples of three and six. Dimensions chosen this way can easily be divided by a large number of factors without ending up with millimetre fractions.

Cladding (left)

Cladding is the practice of covering one material with another, which in architecture is typically applied to provide a layer that controls the ingress of weather elements. Cladding is typically applied to a curtain-wall system, such as the Montevetro Building in London, England, designed by Richard Rogers Partnership and created by John Robertson Architects, which is clad with glass and Spanish terracotta tiles. A curtain-wall cladding system is a continuous building façade that does not provide structural support. Photographed by Max Alexander.

The golden section or divine ratio has been used to guide the layout of architecture for millennia, from the Parthenon in Athens, Greece, to modern buildings, due to its ability to produce proportions that are pleasing to the eye.

The use of the golden ratio can be seen in the designs of many buildings. The observation deck of the CN Tower in Toronto, Canada (below left) is positioned at 8:13 of its total 553-metre height; the width-to-height ratio of every ten floors of the United Nations building in New York, USA (below centre), is a golden ratio; and Leonardo da Vinci used the golden ratio in the design of Notre Dame in Paris, France (below right).

Tessellation

Tessellation is a repeated geometric design that covers a surface without gaps or overlaps, such as that in the foyer of the Daily Express Building (right), refurbished by JRA and photographed by Max Alexander. Commonly used in wallpaper designs, the use of tessellation provides a seamless pattern so that a group of objects with the same pattern can be arranged to present a cohesive image.

The Daily Express Building (left)

The Grand Foyer of The Daily Express Building in London, England, features bold patterns and surface ornamentation influenced by aerodynamic principles, which were a common theme when it was built in the 1920s.

Newspapers present one of the most dynamic layout environments due to the fast pace of work and the need to fit a lot of information into a very limited space in such a way that it is attractive and accessible, as can be seen in this redesign of *The Times* by design studio Research Studios.

THE TIMES

Au Lecteur!

Eyes weeping an involuntary tear

Flaubert

Bush facing judgment day

Shocker

Teen among 20 killed in Gaza clashes

Nov. 7th 2006

Masthead (above)
The typography was adjusted to have triangular, wedge serifs that make a stronger visual statement.

Typography (left)
Use of a tighter tracking font means that text can fit more comfortably into narrow columns with fewer unsightly breaks or rivers.

Main cover and supplements (below)
A well-organised and compartmentalised design with masthead and main straps at the top presents a distinct hierarchy that contributes to a clean looking cover and is easily transferred to different supplements, while the column structure gives balance.

Banner or streamer A headline across the page top.

Byline The author's name at the top of a story.

Ears The areas either side of the masthead where weather news or other announcements appear.

Jumpline A continuation instruction for a story that jumps to another page, such as 'continued on page 13'.

Kicker A small headline, usually underlined, which is above and to the left of the main head.

Nameplate The block that graphically presents the name, subtitle and date line of a newspaper.

Sidebar A secondary story that supports or provides more information for a main story.

Porkchop or thumbnail A half-column picture.

Standing heads Headlines that do not change.

Tombstone Placing two or more similar sized headlines side by side.

Skyline A banner head that runs over the nameplate.

Spreads (above)

These spreads from *The Times* redesign show the flexibility of the column structure, which can be altered to run from four to six columns. Notice how the gutters between the columns provide a subtle visual break that is sufficient to clearly separate them.

5.7 Magazines

Magazines represent some of the most innovative and creative use of layouts and graphic design, helping to establish usage norms that are subsequently applied in other areas of publication work and appropriated by other disciplines.

Masthead
A bold sanserif masthead reversed out of vibrant red that grabs attention.

Secondary strap
Set in white space, this secondary strap helps balance the asymmetrical bias of the cover image.

Straps
The strap hierarchy has three levels, but does not overload the visual impression of the cover.

Main strap
The main strap counterbalances the masthead and draws attention down the page.

Barcode
The barcode counterbalances the secondary strap.

The Face (above)
Pictured is a cover from *The Face*, a music and fashion magazine (1980–2004) that was a leading reference for youth culture for over two decades. Its cutting edge music and fashion editorial were complemented and elevated through the designs and typography.

Coverlines or cutlines Short lines of copy on the cover to attract buyers.

Deep caption An illustration or photograph description that is an article unto itself.

Entry point A visual device such as a pull quote, sidebar or list to draw readers into a story.

Sidebar Text containing related, complementary information to a story.

Well The magazine section where feature articles are published, usually in the middle.

Grafik, SEA design studio (above)
Pictured is a template design for contemporary graphic design magazine *grafik*, which features vertically aligned, large sanserif type to make a bold, pictureless visual statement.

FHP (left and below)
Pictured are covers from lifestyle magazine *fhp*, created by Studio Output design studio, about the UK city of Nottingham featuring a stylish, modern design with a logo that forms a ligature.

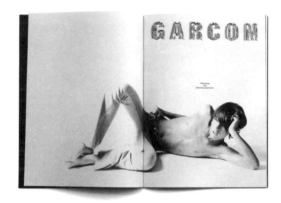

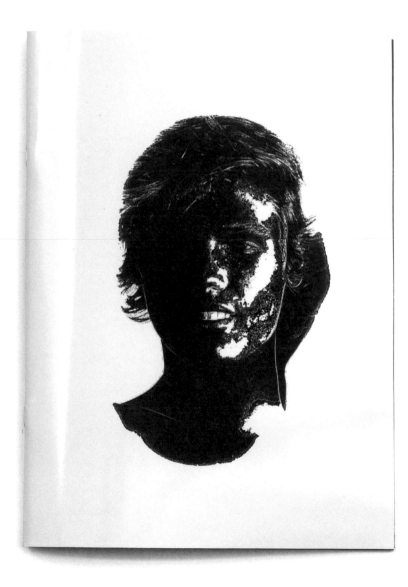

Man Woman Girl Boy (above, right and opposite)
These spreads are from the Garcon part one and part two features in *Man Woman Girl Boy* magazine created by design studio 3 Deep Design and featuring photography by Justin Edward John Smith. The spreads have almost no text to allow the reader's attention to remain with the images. The central gutter is used to create tension by its division of a full-bleed image. In a similar vein, display text is given its own prominent and unencumbered space.

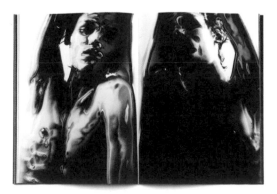

5.8 Books and Brochures

Books and brochures use layout to organise a variety of information. Books tend to be text heavy, although this is far from always the case, while brochures tend to have a more even mix between text and images.

Märkli (above)
This book, created by design studio Frost Design, features front cover and spine text that runs from the head down.

Spine orientation

As books are often stored in bookshelves, it is necessary to identify the book on its spine. Spine text can run up, down or across the spine. Many books feature spine text running from a book's head down so that it can be easily read when the book is lying on its back. However, as the human head turns more easily to the left for vertical reading, this favours text running from the tail up, although this usage may stem from the architect's and engineer's convention that vertical text should be read from the right side of the sheet.

Recto/verso

A spread contains recto and verso folios with the right-hand page being the recto and the left-hand page the verso. The recto page is usually the most dominant in a spread as it is the first page seen when a reader turns over a folio. The eye is naturally drawn to the recto folio and for this reason the right-hand image in the spread below seems dominant. The spread is from a book of advertising images taken by fashion photographer Rankin, created by design studio SEA Design.

Orientation

Orientation

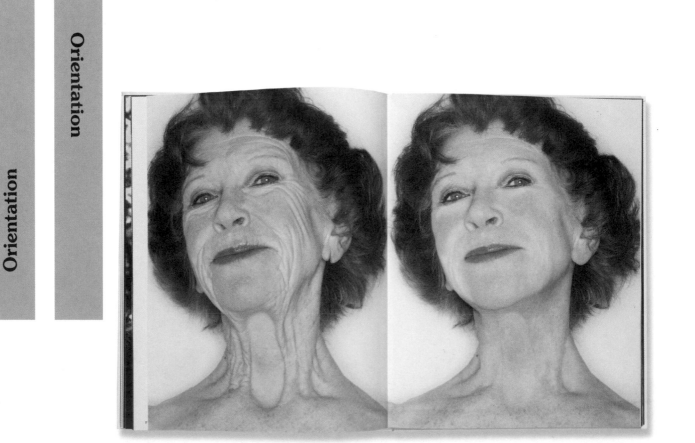

A publication can be enhanced with various additions that add extra pages to a standard publication format. A tip-in is the attachment of a single page by wrapping it around the central fold of a section and gluing along the binding edge, while tipping-on (B) involves pasting a single sheet on to a publication. A throw-out (A) is a folded sheet that extends horizontally and is bound into a publication, while a gatefold (C closed, D open) is a four-panel sheet that is placed in a publication so that its left and right panels fold inwards and meet at the spine.

Pierre Cardin (below)
Pictured is a brochure for fashion designer Pierre Cardin, created by Third Eye design studio, which features a gatefold that allows more garments from the collection to be shown side by side.

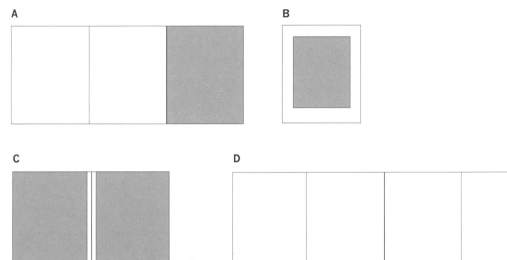

A

B

C

D

Dust jacket A jacket around a hardback publication that originally offered protection against dirt and dust, as the name suggests, but more recently has become an integral graphic extension of the book and a key device for promotion.

Endpaper The heavy cartridge paper pages at the front and back of a hardback book that join the book block to the hardback binding. These sometimes depict maps or feature a decorative colour or design.

Case or edition binding A common hard-cover bookbinding method that sews signatures together, flattens the spine, applies endsheets and head-and-tail bands to the spine. Hard covers are attached, the spine is usually rounded and grooves along the cover edge act as hinges.

**Brick-work
(right and opposite)**
Pictured is *Brick-work: Thinking and Making,* a book published by GTA, Institute for the History and Theory of Architecture, ETH Zurich, which looks at the use of brick in the designs of architectural practice Sergison Bates. The book design is simple and uses monotone colours as an antidote to the glossy monograph, and has short pages that divide the case studies and separate the construction drawings from the model photography. The book was printed in German and English and uses two spine text orientations to visually distinguish between the two.

Flock A speciality cover paper produced by coating the sheet with size in patterns or all over after which a dyed flock powder (very fine woollen refuse or vegetable fibre dust) is applied. Originally intended to simulate tapestry and Italian velvet brocade.

Sewn section Unbound book block that has had its binding edge sewn. The blocks are then sewn together.

Slipcase A protective case for a book or set of books open at one end so that only the book spines are visible.

Buckram A coarse cotton fabric, sized with glue that is used to stiffen garments and to produce cover stock for book binding. In printing and publishing, buckram is used to provide a hard, tactile long-lasting material for case binding.

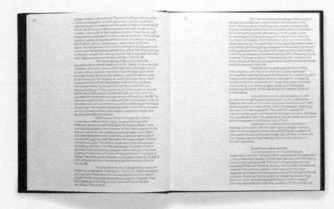 

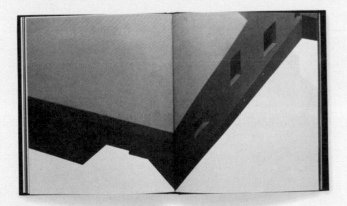 

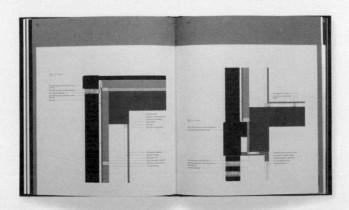

Spreads (above and left)
These spreads from *Brick-work* show a variety of visual treatments for the contents of the book that range from full-bleed imagery extending over both the recto and verso pages, a bank of multiple images, and diagrams of architectural details, all with the same monotone palette colouration, which provides consistency throughout the publication.

Work in progress (above and right)
Pictured is a large-scale magazine about the practice of London architect firm John Robertson Architects, by designer Gavin Ambrose. The publication features a map of London showing the location of some of the projects the practice has worked on, with further details and a thumbnail picture of the building contained in a bar running across the bottom of the spread, which organises the information in a clear and easily accessible manner.

CAPITAL DEVELOPMENTS:
21 BUILDINGS, 13 YEARS

1 Kensington Green, W8
Conversion of the former St Mary Abbot's hospital, a handsome Tudor style block, into apartments.
Client: Taylor Woodrow Capital Developments

2 50 Cannon Street, EC4
Refacing a drab 1970s office in a contemporary idiom within a conservation area gives it a new image and marks the greatly upgraded space within.
Client: Guardian Assurance

3 40 Strand, WC2
Adding a new floor, remodelling the entrance and replacing services repositioned this obsolete 1950s building in the 1990s marketplace.
Client: Land Securities

4 One Great St Helen's, EC3
This neat addition to the urban realm was an early demonstration of the BCO's generic specification.
Client: Greycoat plc

5 City Quay, St Katharine's Dock, E1
JRA's expertise in producing and scheduling information for construction of this large, complex housing scheme.
Client: Taylor Woodrow Capital Developments

11 One Knightsbridge Green, SW1
Remodelling the base of a 1950s 'rent' slab meets modern retail needs and creates an appropriate office entrance.
Client: Prudential Assurance Company Ltd

12 2-5 Old Bond Street, W1
Two high profile retailers recognised the qualities of this 1930s building which JRA's refurbishment unlocked.
Client: Prudential Assurance Company Ltd

13 The Exchange, N8
JRA successfully converted this 1950s telephone exchange to residential by giving it an image which consciously reflects its status as an urban building.
Client: Berkeley Homes

14 One Seething Lane, EC3
A sensitive piece of urban infill, making a contextual and contemporary new office building in a conservation area.
Client: Land Securities

15 City Law Offices, EC2
JRA achieved a sophisticated and contemporary interior for a variety of facilities, using a family of components to control expenditure.
Client: Linklaters

16 10 Queen Street Place, EC4
New technology and targeted structural intervention efficient and flexible modern offices for SJ Berwin dealing floor groundscaper.
Client: The Blackstone Group International

The presentation of different pieces of related information within a design is often achieved through cross-referencing. The different pieces of information in the work below are presented in a consistent and ordered manner in a bar, while a simple numbering system provides cross-referencing in the layout to create connections between the buildings and their locations.

4/5

In first 13 years John Robertson Architects
contributed to commercial, residential and
et life across London. This spread highlights
f some recently completed projects, showing
JRA* (offices located at Bankside near Tate
ern) has found ways of designing new buildings
reconfiguring old ones to optimise value in a
ty of urban situations.

GOING GREEN IN GREENWICH

10 QUEEN STREET PLACE EC4 2/3

COPENHAGEN SOUTH HARBOUR REGENERATION 6/7

1999   2000   2002

7   8   9   10

xpress Building, EC4
jewel of the Daily
kes a focus for the
eadquarters building
ound it.
tochu Corporation

120 Fleet Street, EC4
The second phase of a major North American investment bank's European headquarters comprising 500,000sqft of dealing and office floor space.
Client: The Itochu Corporation

10 Throgmorton Avenue, EC2
Rationalised efficient floorplates lie behind this refurbished historic façade.
Client: The Worshipful Company of Carpenters

Montevetro, SW11
Working in collaboration with Richard Rogers Partnership JRA developed the detailed design and construction methods for one of London's most striking residential buildings.
Client: Taylor Woodrow Capital Developments

190 High Holborn, WC1
A strong new entrance hall concept shows how targeted interventions can transform identity.
Client: Land Securities

18   19   20   21

Millennium Village, SE10
n for high density, sustainable
ing.
Ltd

20 Cursitor Street, EC4
A carefully considered façade gives identity and brings amenity to this office building within in a tight urban grain.
Client: Morley Fund Management

107 Cheapside, EC2
A JRA hallmark is to bring a new life to outmoded buildings through targeted and innovatively designed interventions and additions. This design extends and refurbishes a 1950s building to increase the quantity, quality and flexibility of space. Rational floorplates are easy to layout and divide, while up to eight retail units help to animate the street and contribute to the overall transformation of Cheapside.
Client: The Carlyle Group

Park House, Finsbury Circus, EC2
Two Grade II listed buildings will be subsumed within a new development. A huge uplift in floor area comes from a rear extension, making large floorplates around a central atrium.
Client: Prudential Assurance Company Ltd

16 Great Queen Street, WC2
Remodelling the façade, reorganising the interiors and improving the surrounding public realm means this 1958 office block will provide high quality contemporary interiors with the added benefits of an attractive setting.
Client: Henderson Global Investors

5.9 Packaging

Packaging design is one of the most dynamic areas of graphic design as it can make all the difference between the product it protects selling or not, while dealing with the complication that design has to be transposed on to a three-dimensional surface.

Packaging layout needs to present information clearly and define a visual space for the product that meets the tastes of the market. Perfume packaging, such as that featured here, competes in some of the most demanding retail settings, including department stores, duty-free shops and boutiques, and has to work vigorously for shopper attention. The printing is luxurious, but a design has a very limited space to work in due to the confines imposed by the box construction, which also limits the space available to create a visual hierarchy.

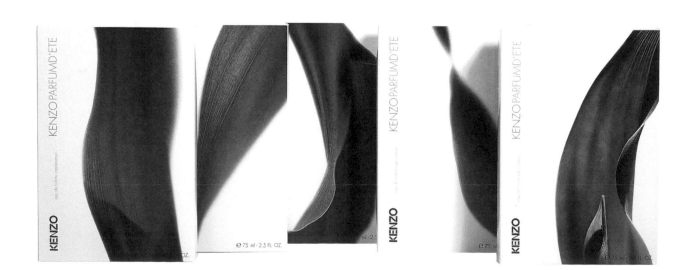

Kenzo (above and opposite)

This spread features packaging created by Research Studios design studio for Kenzo, which features simple natural beauty emphasised by white space. The box panels (left, bottom) that feature a turning green leaf and the growing red poppy (above) present a narrative that utilises the physical packaging and provides product colour coding, which helps consumer recognition and aids repeat purchase.

Photodisc (right)

The Photodisc CD packaging by Getty design studio features one image from the photographs contained on each CD that is creatively cropped to give each layout a modernist tension. The layout does not feature labelling, other than the company brand, as the images act as visual clues to the content, clearly distinguishing between a CD of photographs and one of illustrations.

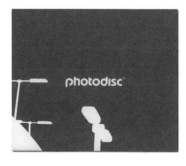

Lascivious (left)
This look book created by design studio Third Eye Design for Lascivious features an oversize outer providing generous flaps, which turn the product into a self-packaged item. The simple layout aids product identification and complements the large format with large photographs presented with passepartouts that maintain a sense of scale in the publication.

Kshocolât (right)
Pictured is product packaging by Third Eye Design for Scottish chocolate manufacturer Kshocolât that features a simple layout aided with colour coding for both tins and bars to ease product identification, which also gives a distinctive look to the brand.

5.10 Websites

Websites were initially built as electronic versions of a publication, but as the technology for building them has become increasingly powerful and sophisticated, Web designers are able to create Web layouts that are more elaborate and function in different ways.

Fixed or scrolling

A Web designer can determine the format of the website as a fixed or scrolling screen, or a combination thereof. A fixed screen gives more control and acts more like a physical paper publication, while a scrolling screen can provide a page of infinite dimension that arguably allows for a more democratic presentation, as the user exercises more control over the delivery of information.

Nick Cobbing (right)

This is the website of photographer Nick Cobbing, created by designer Diarmuid Slattery, which presents images within a fixed screen so that they resemble large-format prints.

Million Dollar home page (opposite)

Alex Tew took the idea of the pixel as the basic grid structure to an extreme through the creation of the Million Dollar home page as he sought to earn $1 million by selling one million pixels for $1 each to pay for his university education. The resulting layout is chaotic, postmodern, even deconstructionist, as it operates at different scales, with a plethora of odd-shaped vertical and horizontal blocks that can link to other sites.

Policemen wearing PLA uniforms read together outside the Jokhang Temple / Tibetans Story   2 / 6

Cookie crumb

Even simple websites can provide a means for the viewer to return to previously viewed screens by using Web cookies that track and maintain user information. A cookie is a piece of text sent by a server to a Web browser and then returned unchanged each time the browser accesses the server. This functions like the trail of cookie crumbs left by Hansel and Gretel. A cookie crumb trail for this page could read something like the text below:

Design is now largely performed on computers with information rendered in pixels. The number of pixels that a screen can show affects the resolution of an image and in some ways acts as a grid upon which information is presented. The importance of the pixel as the basic building block for graphic design has increased with the rise of the Internet.

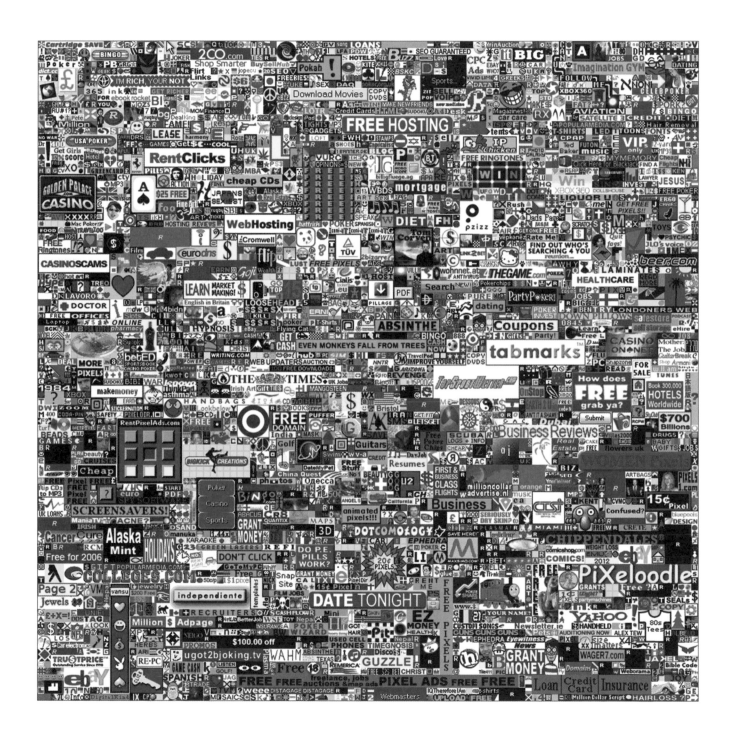

A translational website appropriates the structure of other media and transposes it on to the Web. A poster or map may not be the most logical starting point for a website design, but animated scrolling can add a dynamic touch and sense of exploration to the overall presentation, as shown in the example below.

Studio Thomson website (www.studiothomson.co.uk)
This is the website of Studio Thomson design studio and features a structure that encourages the viewer to explore examples of its work. The initial poster presentation of its different categories or chapters gives multiple directions or paths to follow. The connections that the user can make are more varied and removed from the pattern that would be enforced by a linear narrative.

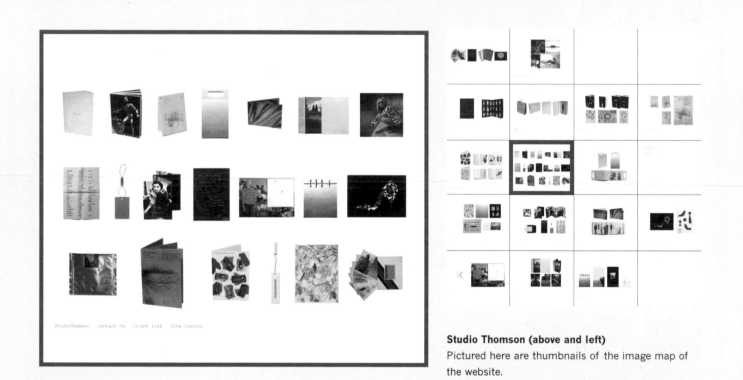

Studio Thomson (above and left)
Pictured here are thumbnails of the image map of the website.

Coordinates

The Studio Thomson design studio website has a structure that encourages the viewer to explore examples of its work. Multiple directions or paths can be followed that are accessed through a textless, visual key arranged like a map of city blocks. Using Flash technology, clicking on an item sends the viewer on a journey through the various blocks until the selected item arrives on screen. Even with just 19 items, there are dozens of 'journeys' possible. Each piece has specific x and y coordinates that reinforce the map analogy.

Map analogy
A map is a pictorial device that allows a viewer to get their bearings for a place and navigate their way from one location to another. A map provides an element of containment and structure to information, which provides the reader with freedom and an ability to explore with a reduced likelihood of getting lost.

A linear narrative presents the viewer with a logical starting or entrance point from which follows a prescribed journey through a carefully selected and positioned sequence of pages or images. The linear narrative is almost cinematic in that the message or story unfolds frame by frame, with the viewer unable to alter the sequence or the way in which the content is viewed, such as in the Studio Myerscough website presented here. The advantage is that the person, artist or design agency that uploads the information controls its presentation order.

Studio Myerscough website (www.studiomyerscough.co.uk)
These are images from the website of Studio Myerscough design studio, which uses a linear structure to showcase 24 work examples. This layout structure, dominated by large-scale images presented with passepartouts, allows for the presentation of a diverse and varied selection of projects without the need to compartmentalise them into a specific order or overriding thematic structure, which results in an unexpected juxtaposition of ideas that the viewer scrolls through. This removal of order ties into how the multi-disciplinary studio positions itself in the design community through the production of exciting and engaging works in many fields. The 24 images can be viewed passively by scrolling through one after the other, or a more active approach can be taken by going back and forth to compare the images.

Linear narrative
A linear narrative presents the viewer with a sequence of selected pages positioned and controlled by the creator to tell a particular story. The level of control that the narrative creator applies over the Roman road can be very strict or allow the user to take some control. In a website presentation, the viewer may only be allowed to advance sequentially through all the images or may be given the chance to flip back and forth through the sequence or even jump ahead randomly to different pages within it.

Studio Myerscough (above and left)
The images below show the sequence construction that presents the viewer with a prescribed order. The qualities of one image contrast with and relate to the succeeding image in the chain. Although each scene is viewed in isolation, they are part of a larger meta-narrative that extends throughout the sequence, in a similar relationship to that between a movie still and the complete film.

Roman-road analogy
The Roman civilisation was noted for the long, straight roads it constructed to link the various territories of its empire. Websites can present a visual analogy of a Roman road due to the infinite number of pages that can be created, which effectively stretch onwards in one long, never-ending line.

Translational – The Magazine and the Book

A website can be a magazine with a limitless number of sections or chapters that the viewer can thumb through. Each section of mini narratives, accessed through a header link on the home page, leads into different sections or departments that can contain any number of pages. Unlike a paper-based magazine, there is no overriding structural limitation from the format extent to curtail sections.

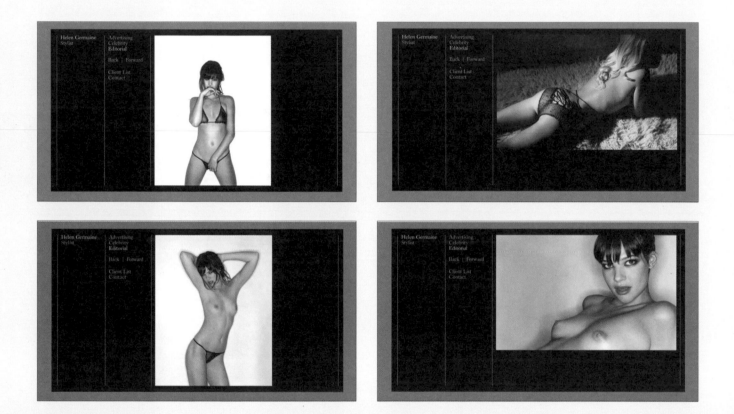

Magazine analogy
Websites can be designed to provide a facsimile of a magazine with content visually presented as magazine pages, which allow the viewer to thumb through them by clicking on the 'forward' and 'back' buttons. However, adding pages does not require page count revision or the need to add a new section as with the imposition of traditional printed matter. This is translational in that elements of the magazine medium are used in a different media, in this instance a website. While each Web page behaves like a traditional page, each one is an unique 'plate' that is viewed in isolation from the others. The viewer is often restricted to viewing them in a predetermined sequence, more so than the structure of a book, which always allows a reader to thumb through it. In essence, it is passive, like watching a film, with the viewer only able to make decisions at the main junctions.

This is the website for stylist Helen Germaine, designed by James Groves at George & Vera design studio. The site features several series of images, each presented as a separate 'Roman road', which are accessed from the home page through various subject headings.

The home page acts as a crossroads or entry point to the site, sometimes called a lid, within which the various roads or subject headings are provided. The content of the site is to be viewed, rather than read, and the images are displayed in a way that resembles magazine spreads, the medium for which many of the images were originally intended, complete with black passepartout presentation that gives them space to breathe in the open layout design.

Pictured below are thumbnails of the various chapters or roads the website presents that are of uneven length. However, one of the advantages of the Web medium is that different extents can be accommodated without any physical impact to the final result.

Image sequences (below)
Pictured here are thumbnails of the image sequences of the main editorial sections of the website.

Home page

Advertising

Celebrity

Editorial

Client list

Contact

5.11 The Built Environment

The built environment around us is an all-encompassing layout from street and building planning to the signage that guides us through it. Layouts that provide easily accessible information and allow rapid transport and communication are essential to densely populated societies.

Signage (above)
Pictured is signage for the Barbican arts centre in London, England, created by Cartlidge Levene in association with design studio Studio Myerscough, and a fold-out map of the venue.

Layout in the environment can be seen in practice in most public spaces. These typically have identified entrance, exit and circulation routes, such as a fire escape, which benefits from both wayfinding and signage.

Signage Signage is any structure or display found on a building or in the street that communicates information to the general public.

Wayfinding Wayfinding is the ability of a person to find his or her way to a given destination using information in a building's design, such as halls and walkways that aid orientation, in addition to signage.

Signage (right and below right)
The large-scale Barbican signage is like an art installation, as well as providing much-needed information for visitors.

Floor plans (below)
Pictured are the Barbican floor plans as featured on the fold-out guide map shown opposite.

WalkRide (above and right)

Pictured is *WalkRide*, an identity created by design studio Cartlidge Levene in collaboration with City ID for an information and movement system for Newcastle–Gateshead in England, which combines information for pedestrians and public transport users. The identity reflects the culture and heritage of the area, while providing the flexibility to express complex practical information via maps and bus timetables, to more expressive elements such as bus livery.

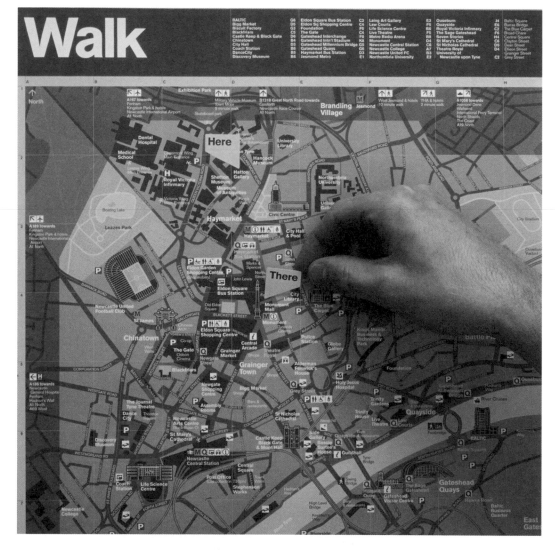

Using charts and graphs to present quantitative information is a simple, effective and very visual way of presenting and organising the information within a layout.

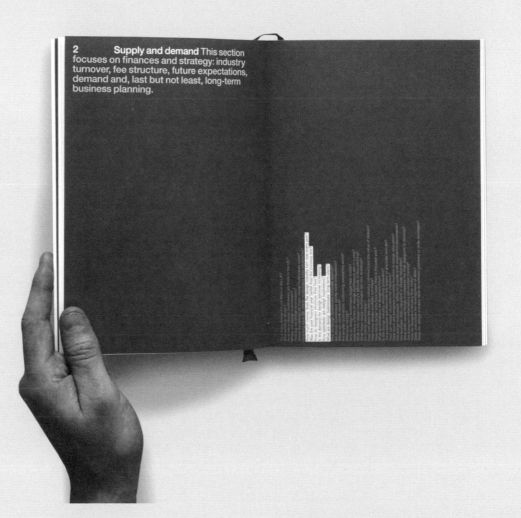

The Business of Design (above, right and below)
Pictured is *The Business of Design*, a UK Design Council publication that presents the results of a design industry survey. The use of a simple typographic grid and a range of chart styles presents data in a simple and user-friendly way that gives readers the option of using the document as an in-depth reference book or skim reading it for key facts.

5.13 Identity Programmes

Layout plays a fundamental role in the development of identity programmes to give an organisation an unified approach to external and internal communications. Relationships between similar design elements can easily be maintained by applying a layout to different media and formats.

Identity (right)
This identity for University College for the Creative Arts in England was created by Blast design studio and features a double-C logo that provides the unifying factor over a range of different communication media, from business cards to advertisements, posters and signage. Note that the standard business card design is adapted for use by different departments through the application of different colour schemes and features passepartouts of students' work.

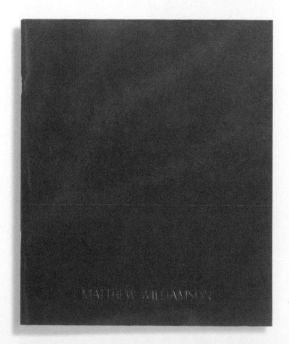

Matthew Williamson (left)
Pictured is an identity created for couture fashion designer Matthew Williamson by design studio SEA Design. The brochure uses a highly reflective cover that alludes to the qualities of silk. It features images of models posed to appear elongated, which reinforces the brand identity contained in the elongated ascender and descender strokes of the typography.

Fonts are sometimes developed under a commission to create something new and unique for a particular organisation to use as part of its identity. While potentially expensive and time consuming, this provides a tailor-made solution to the challenge of creating an identity. Bespoke fonts often have to work well at display sizes so that they can attractively dominate a layout.

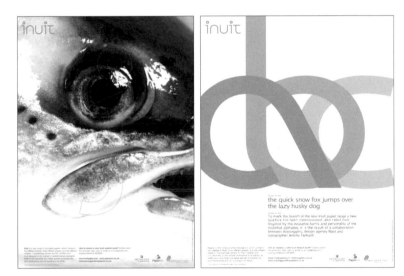

Inuit (above, right and below)
This is Inuit, a bespoke font inspired by the evocative forms of the Inuktitut alphabet, created by typographer Jeremy Tankard and Blast design studio for the Inuit paper range of paper manufacturer Arjowiggins. The unusual forms of the unique font help form the brand identity and create eye-catching areas of colour when used at large typesizes.

Somerset House (above)
Pictured are promotional items created by design studio Research Studios for Somerset House in London, England that feature a die-cut mirror placed *in situ* to reflect the beauty and history of the building. This blurs the boundary between the formal and the informal, design and art, object and subject.

etc. venues (right and below)

An identity that is used across a range of different formats and media depends on layout to establish continuity between the different pieces. Pictured are examples from an identity created by Blast design studio for etc. venues that is used for print and Web communications, interior signage and promotional objects, such as bottles. The identity functions due to the visual impact of the typeface and this is maintained from one medium to the next by its application in the layout of the different items.

instigate,
debate,
listen,
create **etc.**

This volume discusses layout principles and methods that are applicable to a wide variety of media. As this book presents many different methods for creating layouts, it is pertinent to detail various standards or norms that are used by the printing and graphic arts industries, some of which are regulated by international norms.

This chapter details common standards that govern paper and book sizes, CD and DVD formats, outdoor media and stationery in the UK, various European countries and North America as a ready-reference.

This chapter will look at:

Standard paper sizes provide a convenient and efficient means for designers and printers to communicate with each other.

The practical benefits of standardising paper sizes have been recognised for centuries and its practice has a history that can be traced back to 14th-century Italy. The ISO system is based on a height-to-width ratio of the square root of 2 (1:1.4142), which means that each size differs from the next or previous by a factor of 2 or 1/2.

ISO standard (right)
The ISO standard provides for a range of complementary paper sizes to cater for most common printing needs, as shown in this table.

Size	Standard use
A0, A1	Posters and technical drawings, such as blueprints
A1, A2	Flip charts for meetings
A2, A3	Diagrams, drawings and large tables and spreadsheets
A4	Magazines, letters, forms, leaflets, photocopiers, laser printers and general usage
A5	Notepads and diaries
A6	Postcards
B5, A5, B6, A6	Books
C4, C5, C6	Envelopes to enclose A4 letters: unfolded (C4), folded once (C5), folded twice (C6)
B4, A3	Newspapers. These sizes can be handled by many photocopying machines
B8, A8	Playing cards

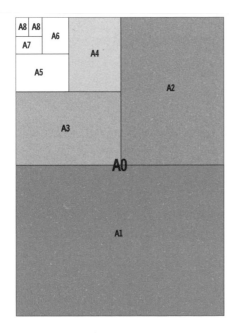

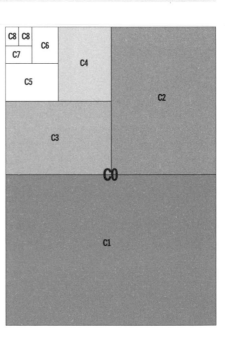

A series

Format	[mm]
A0	841 x 1189
A1	594 x 841
A2	420 x 594
A3	297 x 420
A4	210 x 297
A5	148 x 210
A6	105 x 148
A7	74 x 105
A8	52 x 74
A9	37 x 52
A10	26 x 37

B series

Format	[mm]
B0	1000 x 1414
B1	707 x 1000
B2	500 x 707
B3	353 x 500
B4	250 x 353
B5	176 x 250
B6	125 x 176
B7	88 x 125
B8	62 x 88
B9	44 x 62
B10	31 x 44

C series

Format	[mm]
C0	917 x 1297
C1	648 x 917
C2	458 x 648
C3	324 x 458
C4	229 x 324
C5	162 x 229
C6	114 x 162
C7/6	81 x 162
C7	81 x 114
C8	57 x 81
C9	40 x 57
C10	28 x 40
DL	110 x 220

The ISO standard paper sizes are used throughout the world with the exception of the system used by the USA and Canada, where many formats are regulated by American National Standards.

The most commonly used sizes, letter, legal, executive and ledger/tabloid, are pictured below, together with their specifications.

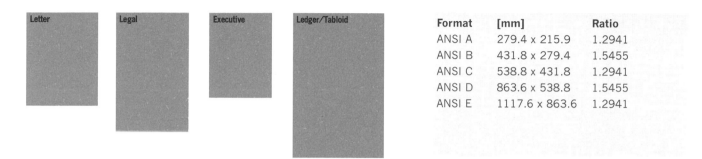

Format	[mm]	Ratio
ANSI A	279.4 x 215.9	1.2941
ANSI B	431.8 x 279.4	1.5455
ANSI C	538.8 x 431.8	1.2941
ANSI D	863.6 x 538.8	1.5455
ANSI E	1117.6 x 863.6	1.2941

US system

As with the ISO paper size system, the US/Canadian method maintains a relationship in the ratios of the sizes. However, while the ISO system enjoys a uniform aspect ratio, the US system alternates between two: 17/11=1.545 and 22/17=1.294, which means one cannot reduce or magnify from one format to the next without leaving a vacant margin.

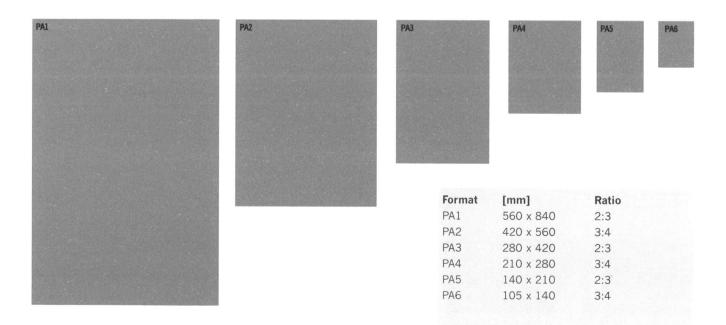

Format	[mm]	Ratio
PA1	560 x 840	2:3
PA2	420 x 560	3:4
PA3	280 x 420	2:3
PA4	210 x 280	3:4
PA5	140 x 210	2:3
PA6	105 x 140	3:4

Canadian system

Canadian standard CAN 2-9.60M, introduced in 1976, defines six P formats that are rounded versions of the US sizes. As with their US counterparts, the Canadian sizes lack a common height/width ratio and they differ from what the rest of the world uses.

The ISO standard paper sizes were based on the Deutsche Industrie Norm standard DIN 476 from 1922. Deutsche Institut für Normung (DIN) is the German Institute for Standardisation, which has been influential in the establishment of many standards used around the world today, including paper standards. Perhaps the most well-known is DIN 476, which was the standard that introduced what became the A4 paper size in 1922, which was subsequently adopted as ISO 216 in 1975.

1451 – a typeface

DIN (above and below right)
Pictured above is a German car licence plate. DIN 1451 was used on licence plates until it was replaced in November 2000 by FE Schrift, which was designed for better tamper resistance and easier automatic character recognition.

Pictured are FF DIN (top) and DIN 1451 MittelSchrift (bottom). FF DIN was re-cut to be used by the print industry due to the popular appeal of DIN 1451. Note how DIN 1451 occupies less space than FF DIN.

DIN 1451
DIN 1451 is a sanserif typeface standard established in 1936 that is used in traffic, administration and business applications. Commonly seen on Germany's road and rail signs due to its legibility, its origins go back to a type sheet defined by the Prussian rail network in 1906. This typeface captured the attention of the viewer while imparting a contemporary, but ordered feel. DIN 1451 was re-cut as FF DIN to meet the needs of the print market due to interest from graphic designers around the world, and the public at large, in German precision engineering and standards.

ABCDE1234

ABCDE1234

The German standard DIN 476 was published in 1922 and is the original specification of the ISO A and B sizes. However, it has two main differences from its international successor. DIN 476 provides an extension to formats larger than A0, which is indicated by a prefix. These are 2A0, which is twice the area of A0, and 4A0, which is four times A0.

476 – paper sizes

DIN 476 (below)

Pictured are the additional formats contained in DIN 476: 2A0, which is 1,189mm x 1,682mm, and 4A0, which is 1,682mm x 2,378mm.

DIN 824

DIN standard DIN 824 outlines a method for folding standard A0 paper size down to the A4 size. This folding method produces a 20mm margin on one layer that can be used for punching holes for filing so that a document can be unfolded and folded again without it needing to be removed from where it is stored. This method also means that the label field located in the bottom left-hand corner of technical drawings ends up on top of the folded page in the file. The illustrations show how an A0 sheet is folded according to this norm with the highlighted page being the A4 page that remains on the top that is actually 190mm wide (210mm – 20mm).

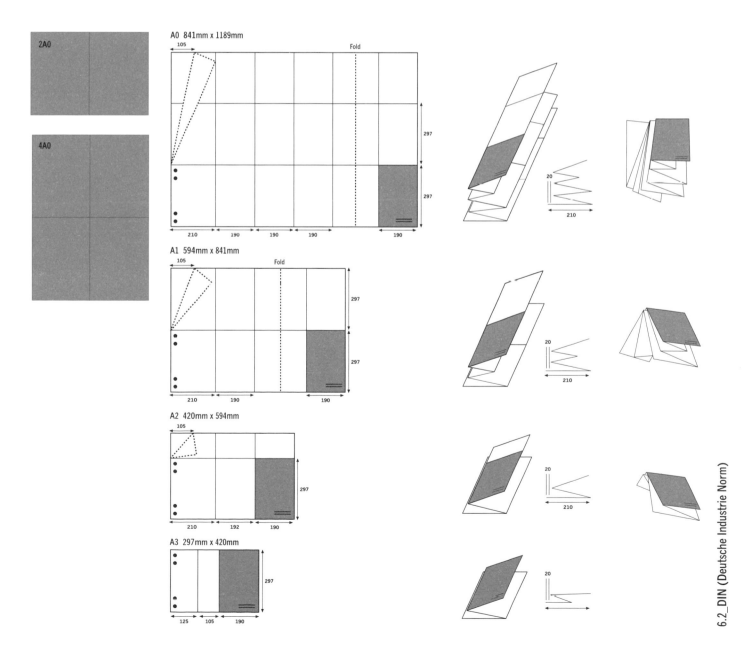

6.3 ISO Envelope Sizes

The ISO standards system provides the C series for envelope sizes, but there is no international standard for window envelopes and matching letterhead layouts. Various national standards exist that are all slightly different, as shown in the table below and the illustrations across this spread.

DL vs. C6/C5 (below)
The slightly larger C6/C5 envelope means that a folded A4 sheet has a more generous fit than a DL envelope provides.

Format	Size [mm]	Content format
C6	114 x 162	A4 folded twice = A6
DL	110 x 220	A4 folded twice = 1/3 A4
C6/C5	114 x 229	A4 folded twice = 1/3 A4
C5	162 x 229	A4 folded once = A5
C4	229 x 324	A4
C3	324 x 458	A3
B6	125 x 176	C6 envelope
B5	176 x 250	C5 envelope
B4	250 x 353	C4 envelope
E4	280 x 400	B4

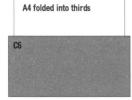

A4 folded into thirds
DL

A4 folded into thirds
C6

DL DIN lang

The DL format (dimension lengthwise according to ISO 269) is the most widely used business letter format of 110mm x 220mm and can take an A4 sheet folded into thirds. The dimensions of this standard are somewhat outside the ISO system, with equipment manufacturers complaining that it is a little too small to deliver reliable automatic envelope fulfilment. German standard DIN 678 was produced to solve this conflict and introduced the C6/C5 format as an alternative to the DL envelope.

United Kingdom: BS 4264

The window of a UK envelope begins 53mm from the top and 20mm from the left margin.

53mm

20mm

93 x 39mm

Switzerland

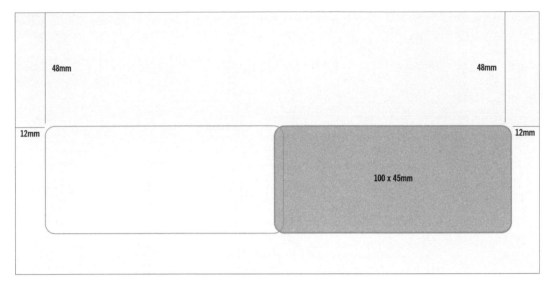

The window of a Swiss envelope begins 48mm from the top and 12mm from either the left or right margin.

Finland

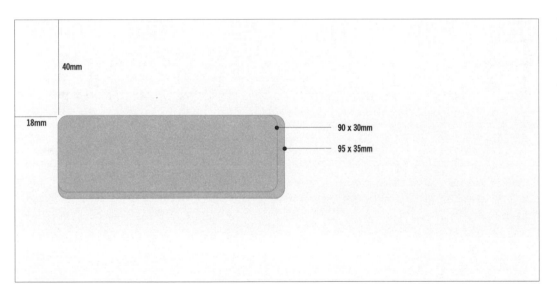

The window of a Finnish envelope (either 95 x 35mm or 90 x 30mm) begins 40mm from the top and 18mm from the left margin.

Germany

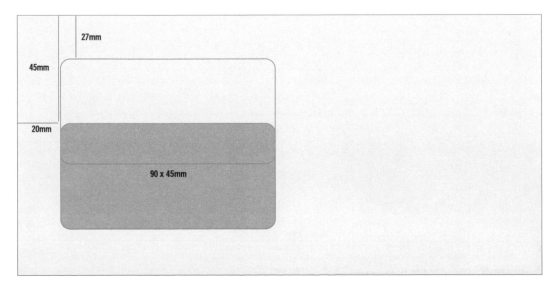

The window of a German envelope begins either 27mm or 45mm from the top and 20mm from the left margin.

In the UK, BS 4264 defines the specifications for DL envelope windows. It specifies that a window should be 93 x 39mm with its top left corner located 20mm from the left margin and 53mm from the top margin of the envelope. BS 1808 specifies an 80 x 30mm address panel for the letterhead with its top left corner to be located 20mm from the left margin and 51mm from the top margin of the page so that it will show through the transparent window of the DL envelope. This panel is embedded inside a 91 x 48mm exclusion zone whose top left corner is located 20mm from the left margin and 42mm from the top margin producing 9mm of space above and below, and an 11mm space to the right of the address panel that should be without any other printing. The manner in which these envelope and letterhead specifications combine is illustrated below.

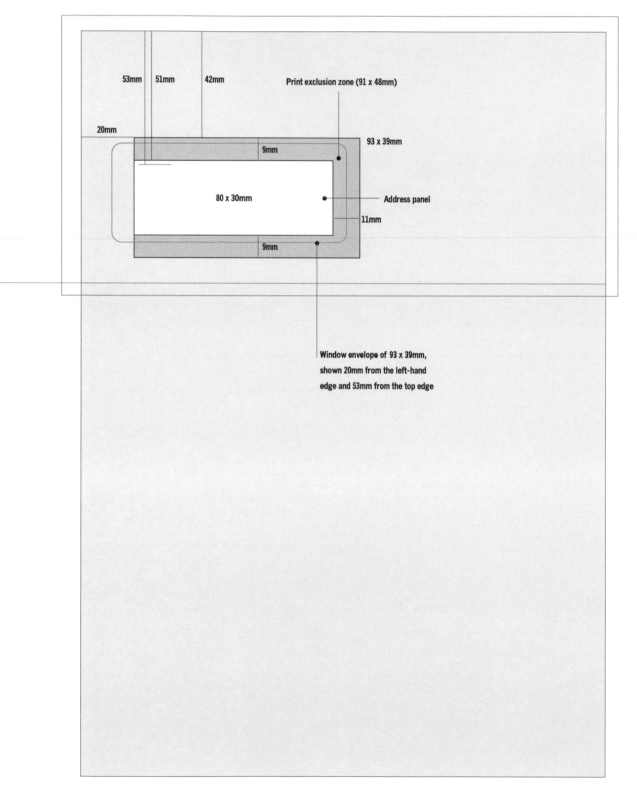

53mm 51mm 42mm Print exclusion zone (91 x 48mm)

20mm

9mm 93 x 39mm

80 x 30mm Address panel

11mm

9mm

Window envelope of 93 x 39mm, shown 20mm from the left-hand edge and 53mm from the top edge

99mm

Switzerland specifies an envelope window of 100 x 45mm to be located 12mm from either the left or the right edge, with a 48mm space from the top (for C6 and C5/C6) or 52mm (for C5). The SNV 010130 letterhead standard (shown below) specifies a 90 x 40mm address panel 45mm from the top and 8mm from the right edge of the A4 page.

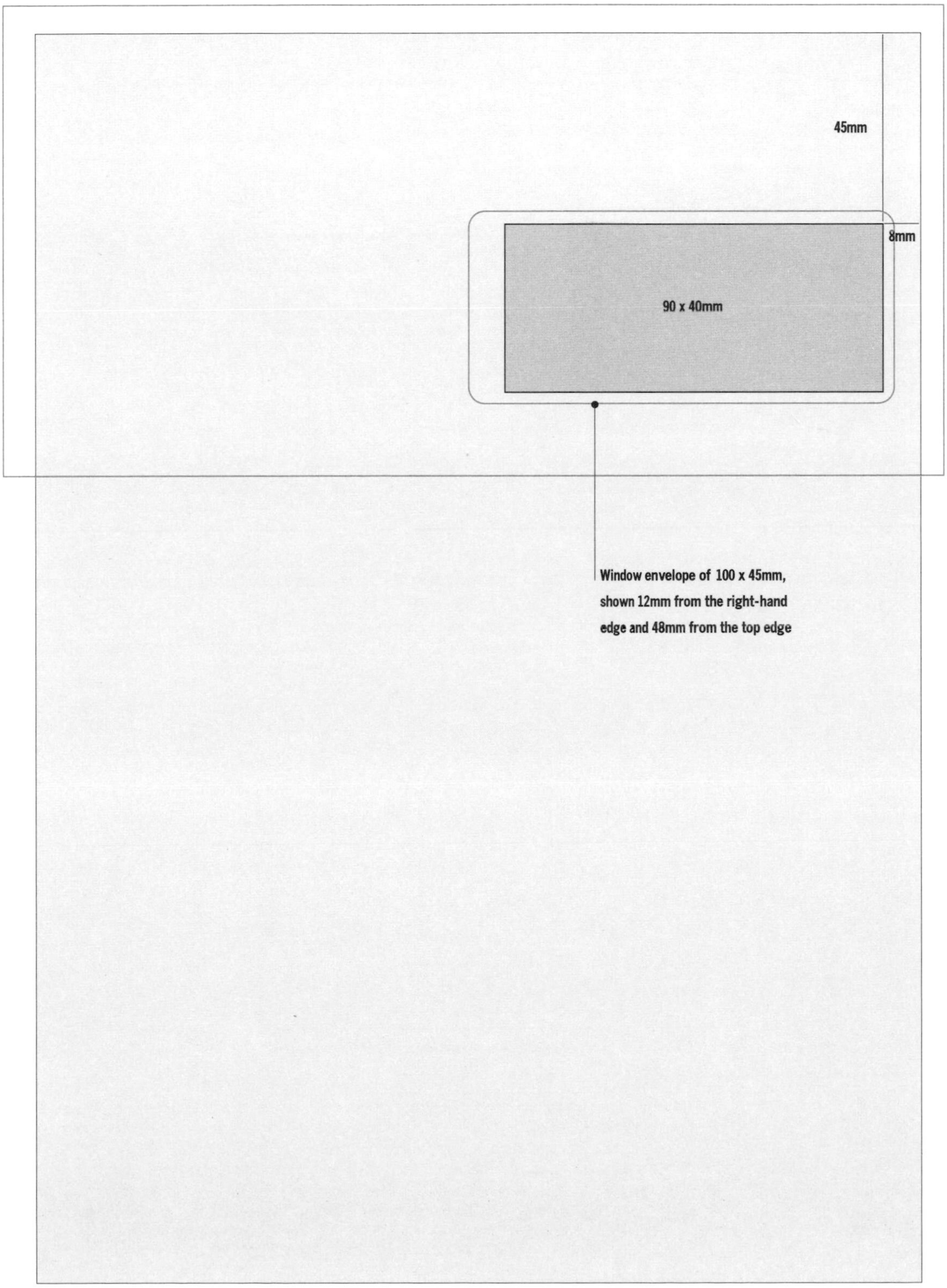

45mm

8mm

90 x 40mm

Window envelope of 100 x 45mm,
shown 12mm from the right-hand
edge and 48mm from the top edge

Through SFS 2488 (1994) Finland specifies a window size of 90 x 30mm for E series envelopes and 95 x 35mm for C series. Both feature an 18mm left margin and 40mm top margin. SFS 2487 (2000) and SFS 2486 (1999) document and form layout specify a 76.2 x 25.4mm address panel located 20mm from the left, and 10±1mm plus 25.4mm from the top.

10mm ± 1mm + 25.4mm

25.4mm reserved for sender's information details

20mm

76.2 x 25.4mm

Window envelope of 95 x 35mm,
shown 18mm from the left-hand
edge and 40mm from the top edge

DIN 680 specifies an address window of 90 x 45mm, 20mm from the left edge and 15mm from the bottom of C6, DL, and C6/C5 envelopes. For C4 envelopes this should be 27mm or 45mm from the top edge. Letterhead standard DIN 676 specifies an 85 x 45mm field visible through the window, with the top 5mm for the sender's address and the bottom 40mm for the recipient's address. This panel starts 20mm from the left edge and 27mm (form A) or 45mm (form B) from the top. Two alternatives allow a choice of a small (form A) or large (form B) letterhead layout in the area above the address field.

Folding marks help insertion of letters into window envelopes, with one (for C6) on the top edge, 148mm from the left edge. Folding marks on the left edge are 105 and 210mm from the bottom (form A) or 105 and 210mm from the top (form B).

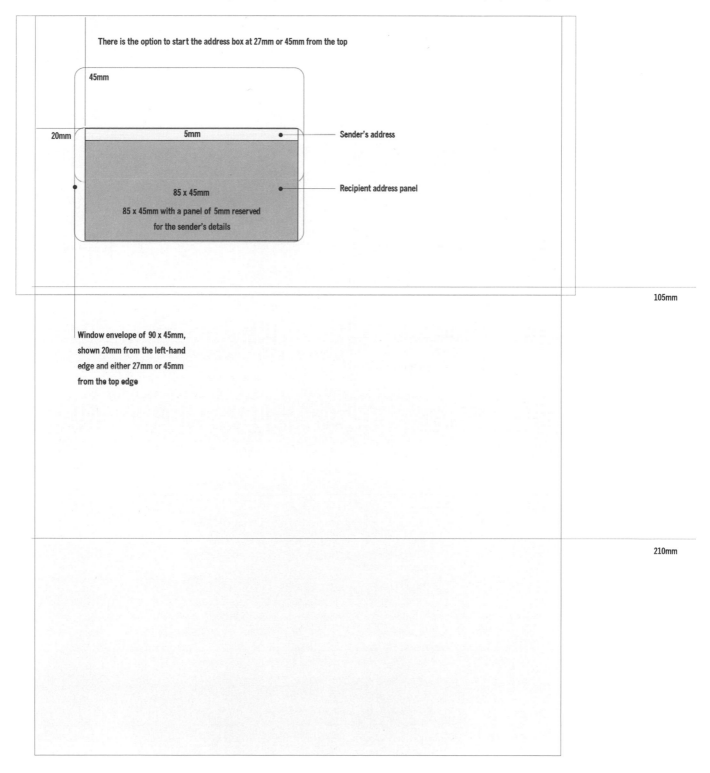

There is the option to start the address box at 27mm or 45mm from the top

45mm

20mm

5mm — Sender's address

85 x 45mm

85 x 45mm with a panel of 5mm reserved for the sender's details

— Recipient address panel

105mm

Window envelope of 90 x 45mm, shown 20mm from the left-hand edge and either 27mm or 45mm from the top edge

210mm

6.4 Book Sizes

Books come in a wide variety of sizes to provide a range of formats so as to handle different types of pictorial and textual content. The proportional variation between the different formats shown in the table below should be considered at the start of the design planning process.

Bound book sizes	Height x width	Bound book sizes	Height x width
1 Demy 16mo	143mm x 111mm	11 Foolscap Quarto (4to)	216mm x 171mm
2 Demy 18mo	146mm x 95mm	12 Crown (4to)	254mm x 191mm
3 Foolscap Octavo (8vo)	171mm x 108mm	13 Demy (4to)	286mm x 222mm
4 Crown (8vo)	191mm x 127mm	14 Royal (4to)	318mm x 254mm
5 Large Crown (8vo)	203mm x 133mm	15 Imperial (4to)	381mm x 279mm
6 Demy (8vo)	213mm x 143mm	16 Crown Folio	381mm x 254mm
7 Medium (8vo)	241mm x 152mm	17 Demy Folio	445mm x 286mm
8 Royal (8vo)	254mm x 159mm	18 Royal Folio	508mm x 318mm
9 Super Royal (8vo)	260mm x 175mm	19 Music	356mm x 260mm
10 Imperial (8vo)	279mm x 191mm		

Standard sizes
The table above details the standard book sizes giving their common names and measurements.

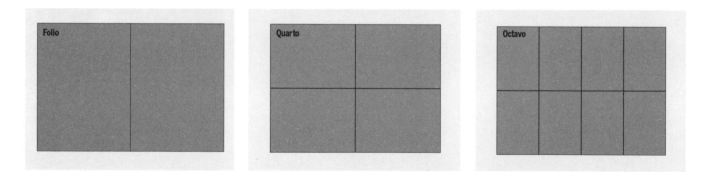

Page sizes (above)
The diagrams show the relative page sizes that can be produced from the same sheet of paper: 16 Crown Folio (381 x 254mm), 4 Crown (8vo) (191 x 127mm) and 12 Crown (4to) (254 x 191mm).

Folio, quarto and octavo
Book size is measured from the head to tail of the spine and from edge to edge across the covers. Two factors affect the size of a book page: the size of the sheet of paper on to which it is printed and the number of times that sheet is folded before it is trimmed. The printing industry defines book sizes in terms of the number of leaves that are created from a standard size sheet of paper for each signature (section) that is printed. Folio editions refer to books made of signatures that have been folded once, quarto editions are formed from signatures folded twice to make four leaves and eight pages, and octavo editions are made from signatures folded three times to give eight leaves and 16 pages. Each leaf is printed on both sides, which means that an octavo signature usually represents 16 pages of the book.

Book sizes were based on standard paper sizes and so there exists a mathematical relationship between them in that successive sizes are either twice or half the area and share one dimension. For example, a Crown folio is 381 x 254mm. With another fold this becomes a Crown quarto measuring 254 x 191mm, and a further fold creates a Crown octavo measuring 191 x 127mm.

Proportion of book sizes (right)

Pictured are scale representations of the various book sizes listed in the table (opposite). The different sizes are proportional due to the relationship between them, which stems from the fact that they are divisions from the same sheet of paper. Crown folio (16) is twice the size of the Crown quarto (12), which is twice the size of the Crown octavo (4).

Page size dictates the space available for a design and has a key influence on the grid that a designer may use to position the elements of a design. The various proportions and sizes that will be used within a design need to be considered at the start of the design planning process so that the correct page size can be chosen for the needs of the job. For example, if wide scholar margins are required, it may be best to select a Foolscap quarto size. As this spread illustrates, grids can be constructed to make use of the available space to position the various design elements.

Page size and layout (right)

These grids are based on Foolscap quarto or 4to (right) and Imperial 4to (below). Although these are very rudimentary sketches, it is possible to see that the page proportions lend themselves to the presentation of different material. For example, a narrow width might suit a novel, while something wider would be more suitable for a photographic journal.

Foolscap quarto

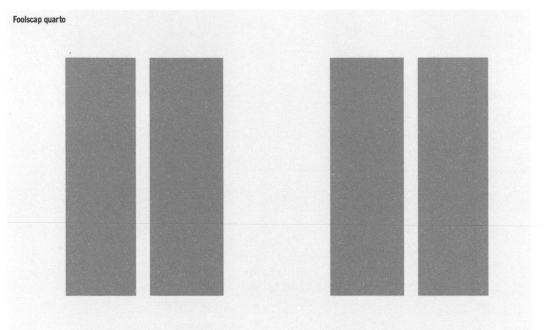

Imperial

The diagrams on this page provide an example of the different ways that images can be presented in a design. While only illustrative, they show how changing the proportions of a page can have more of an impact on the overall design than changing the size of the page *per se*.

Royal 8to

Illustrations (left)
Pictured are a Royal 8to (left) and Demy 16mo (below). The proportions of the Royal 8to lend themselves to the presentation of pictorial information, such as a multitude of photographs, while the squat nature of the Demy 16mo lends itself to use as a brochure, allowing a full-page photograph to be faced with a moderate quantity of text.

Demy 16mo

A Sense of Scale

Scale plays an important role in layout, as viewing distance influences element positioning, typesize and picture size. As this spread shows, designs can be produced with very large and dramatic scales. Producing effective designs for such large scales generally means there is less textual content, as the idea is to catch attention visually.

Single sheet
Size: 762 x 508mm

The basic large-format unit in portrait orientation.

12 sheet
Size: 1,524 x 3,048mm

The 12-sheet poster is a landscape format.

48 sheet
Size: 3,048 x 6,096mm

The standard billboard size gives 200ft² of presentation space in landscape orientation and provides a high level of message frequency.

6 sheet
Size: 1,524 x 1,016mm

This is the most widespread outdoor format in portrait orientation. Its compact size compared to billboards means it can be used in city centres where space is at a premium, such as bus-stops, where it can be found around the world.

Outdoor media comes in a vast range of sizes, from A4 posters to giant billboards. Scale is obviously the defining factor in outdoor media as designs have to catch attention from a distance, which generally means they have dramatic images and minimal text to convey a message.

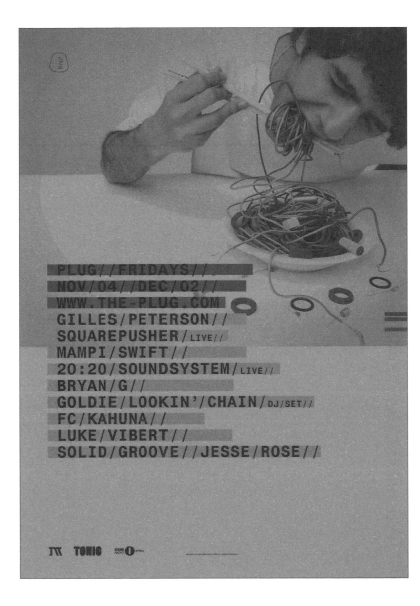

A3 poster (left)

This is a poster created by Peter + Paul design studio for Plug. Given the small size of the poster, creative use of space and a clear text hierarchy were needed to convey the message it contains.

48-sheet large-scale poster (below)

Billboards can be custom made according to the brief, opening up unlimited layout possibilities. Pictured here is an extended billboard for the 'creating new legends' campaign of computer hardware company HP. Four 48-sheet posters were joined together to create a 21-metre-long billboard with the company's Trademark HP crosses elevated above it with thin steel rods to create a flow of crosses up into the sky. At night, these crosses, made with different coloured glitter film, reflected the light of oncoming cars.

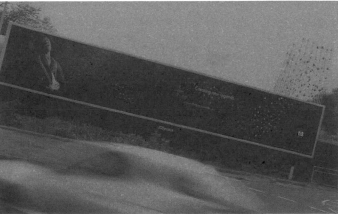

6.6 Standard Templates

Many media that can be printed come in standard sizes, such as CDs and DVDs, which are pictured here. The use of standard sizes allows a graphic designer to maintain an archive of standard templates to use as the starting point for a design.

Standard CD/DVD (right)
The CD/DVD has a 124mm diameter and 118mm that can be printed on with a 40.5mm unprinted internal diameter.

The Mini CD (below)
This has an 85mm diameter and bleed size, with a 79mm artwork area and 18mm unprinted internal diameter.

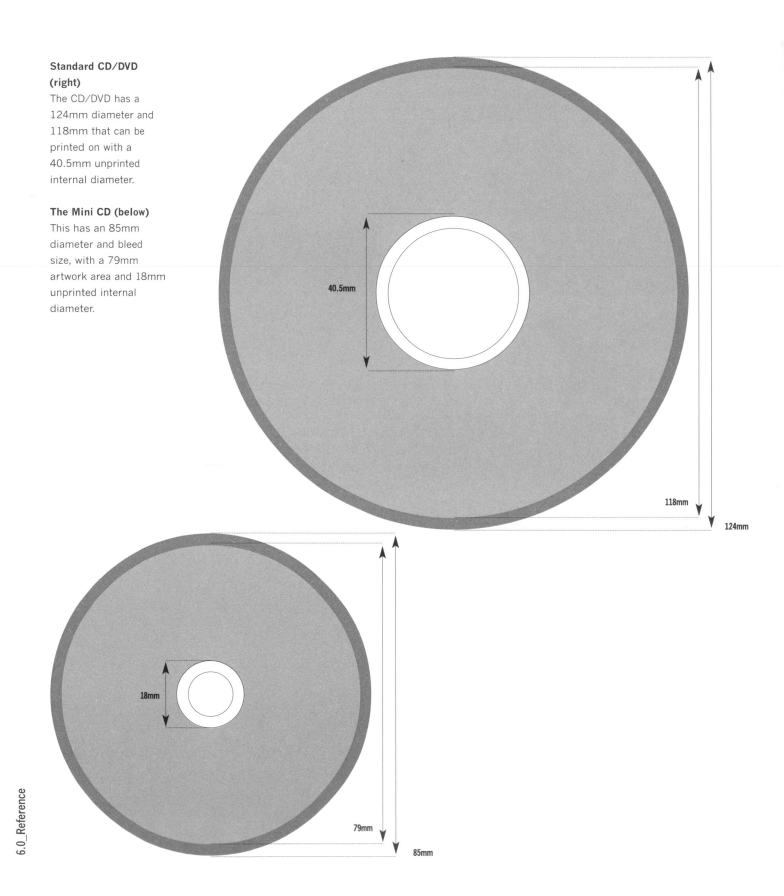

40.5mm

118mm

124mm

18mm

79mm

85mm

CD and DVD printing is often referred to as on-body printing because the image is printed on to the body of the CD. Printing options include screen printing, which is the process used to reproduce full colour for retail CDs such as music. Four-colour lithographic printing gives more resolution and finer colour control than screen printing, with results similar to traditional paper printing.

Full-colour digital printing using inkjet or thermal printers is a low-volume method, but requires white printable CD bodies. Finally, there is black thermal printing that prints black text directly on to the CD. For commercial quantities, the CDs are commonly pre-printed and subsequently duplicated as soon as the master CD is available.

CD/DVD duplication (right)
This shows a CD/DVD duplication that gives full image coverage with an unprinted internal diameter that comes to within 2mm of the central hole.

The business card CD (below)
This has a bleed size of 90 x 64mm and an artwork size of 84 x 58mm with an 18mm unprinted hole. Both shown actual size.

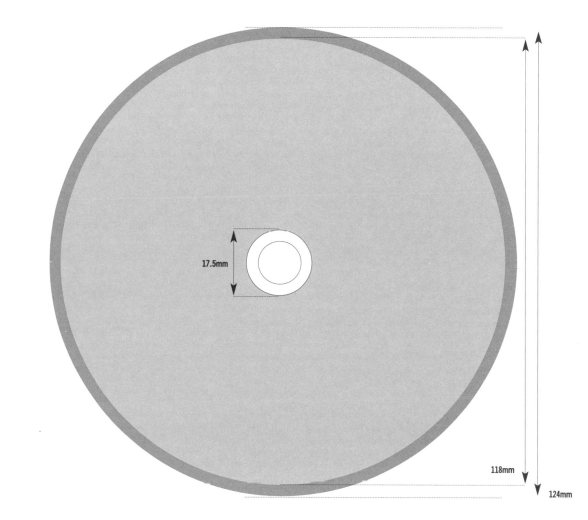

17.5mm

118mm

124mm

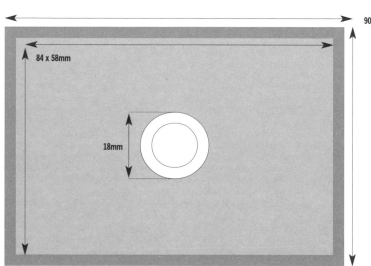

90 x 64mm

84 x 58mm

18mm

CDs and DVDs can be stored in packaging with a range of different formats, such as the wallets and J-cards pictured on this spread. Each format provides a space with slightly different dimensions upon which a design and content information can be placed.

CD wallet (right and below)

This wallet folds in two to provide a simple enclosure to protect a CD/DVD. The wallet is sized to be able to hold a CD tightly so that it does not fall out, but not so tightly that it cannot be easily removed. The wallet provides a 255 x 131mm space for artwork with a finished size of 249 x 125mm, as it includes a 3mm safety border.

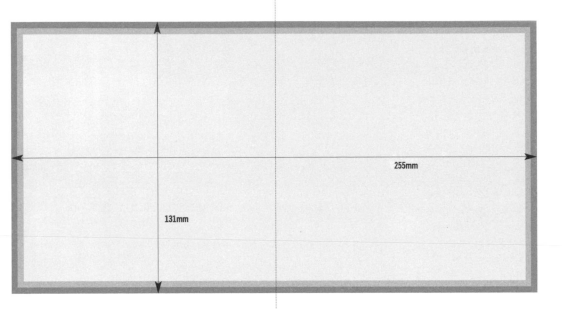

255mm

131mm

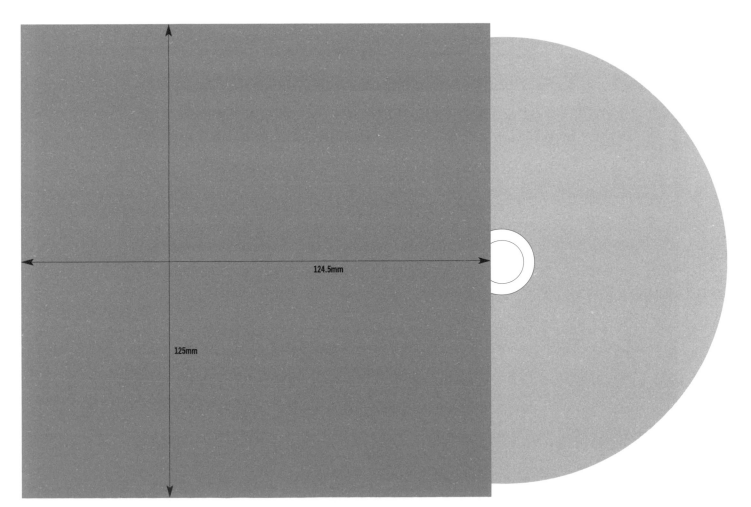

124.5mm

125mm

A CD booklet contains information about the content of a CD, such as the song lyrics for a music album, for example. The overriding format constraint is the size of the CD packaging that it will form part of.

The standard booklet or insert for a CD gives a 120 x 120mm print area that bleeds to 126 x 126mm, with a safety zone of 114 x 114mm. A four-page booklet would require a sheet printing 246 x 126mm including bleed that would then be folded once. A four-page booklet would be printed 246 x 246mm including bleed and would be folded twice, trimmed and saddle-stitched, as shown in the illustration below. It could also be produced without trimming so that the booklet folds out.

**CD booklet
(right and below)**
Pictured is a two-page booklet produced from a 120mm square sheet that can be printed on one or both sides. This gives a safety area of 114 x 114mm, with a 126 x 126mm bleed size and 120 x 120mm trim size. Pictured below is a four-page booklet (top) and an eight-page saddle-stiched booklet (middle) and a fold-out eight-panel poster (bottom).

4pp printed booklet

8pp printed booklet

8pp poster

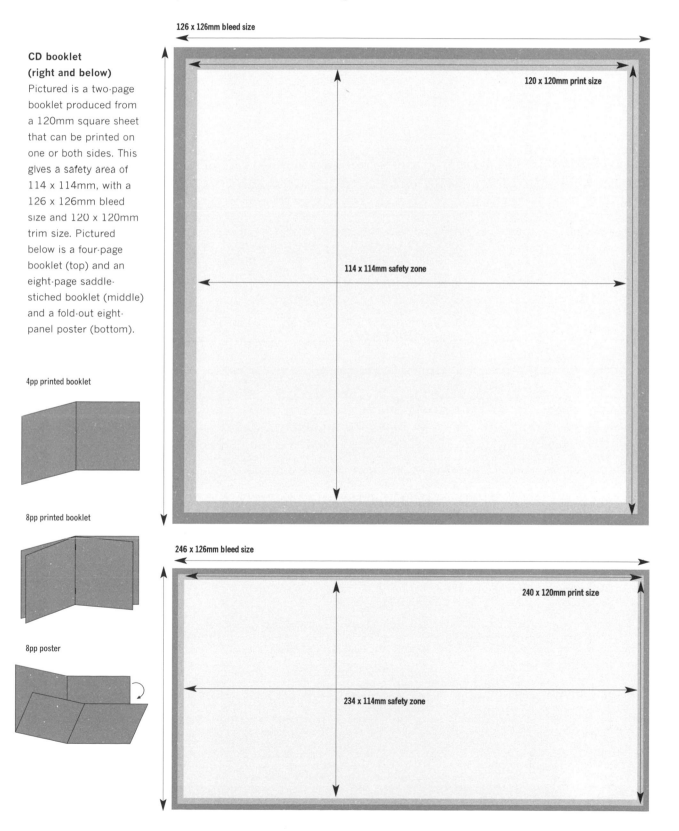

126 x 126mm bleed size

120 x 120mm print size

114 x 114mm safety zone

246 x 126mm bleed size

240 x 120mm print size

234 x 114mm safety zone

CD inlay cards are folios or booklets that are inserted into the packaging of a CD jewel case and contain information about the content, such as the cover artwork for a music CD. Inlays for clear jewel cases tend to be printed double-sided so that information can be read through the transparent case cover, as well as when the case is opened. Single-sided printing is used when the case has a solid colour. Slimline CDs use J-cards, such as the example given below.

CD J-card (above and right)

This is used with a slimline CD jewel case. It is called a J-card because when folded it forms a profile similar to a letter J, as it bends to fit the spine of the case. The J-card has a finished size of 291 x 120.5mm made with a specific die-cut shape. In the diagram the spine is indicated in black.

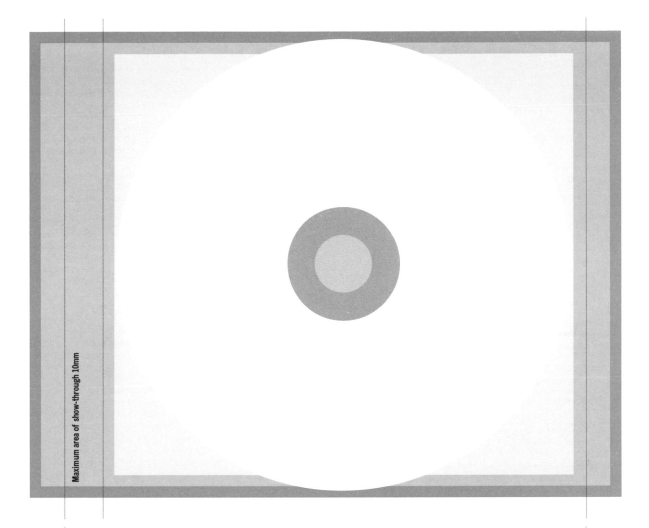

Maximum area of show-through 10mm

Album back inlay (above)

This inlay sits at the back of the jewel case underneath the tray that physically holds the CD. This is typically printed single side and contains the back cover artwork in addition to the two spines. The illustration features an overall size of 156.5 x 128mm with vertical black lines representing the fold marks for the two spines.

Double-sided back inlay

A double-sided back inlay also sits underneath the tray that holds the CD. This inlay has the same dimensions as the album back inlay and also includes the two spines. However, this inlay is printed on both sides as it is for use with a transparent tray and will be visible once the CD is removed. The printed section is not as tall as a CD as this sits in a raised compartment that has a larger size than this part of the packaging.

DVD Case and Packaging

While many DVDs are available in similar jewel cases to CDs, DVD films more commonly use a separate and unique form of packaging that mimics the black plastic boxes of the videotapes that they replaced.

Two-page DVD booklet (right)

Pictured (actual size) is a diagram for a two-page DVD booklet that is printed on a 125 x 175mm sheet. This can be printed on one or both sides and features a 3mm bleed and a 3mm safety zone. Artwork for a four-page booklet is 250mm wide and then folded in two to give panels of this size.

DVD inlay cover wrap (opposite top)

Pictured is a DVD inlay cover wrap that is inserted between the black DVD box and the transparent cover of a standard case, which includes a 14mm spine. This inlay provides an artwork area of 272.3 x 185mm, bleed area of 278.3 x 191mm and a safety zone of 266.3 x 179mm.

Slimline inlay wrap (opposite bottom)

The slimline inlay wrap is similar to the standard inlay, but has a thinner 7mm spine. This gives an artwork area of 265 x 185mm, bleed area of 271 x 191mm, and a safety zone of 259 x 179mm.

131 x 181mm bleed size

125 x 175mm print size

119 x 169mm safety zone

14mm spine

7mm spine

In addition to letters and envelopes, other stationery items are commonly required, such as visiting and business cards, and compliment slips. A compliment slip or thank you note is mailed with a brochure or other item to express gratitude for a service or business received and is typically a replica of the organisation's letterhead. The DL and A6 sizes are used in the UK. DL obviously relates to a standard letterhead size, while the A6 alternative offers a less formal approach in addition to being the standard postcard size.

Visiting or calling cards first appeared in 15th-century China. In Europe, they were delivered by the footmen of aristocrats to announce their arrival to their hosts and contained nothing more than their name. These have evolved into business cards that include full contact details.

210 x 99mm

DL

148 x 105mm

A6

DL and A6 (right and top)
The DL slip has the same width as an A4 sheet of paper and about one third of its height, and fits neatly into a standard business envelope of the corresponding C-series. Compared to this, the A6 slip is a rather unconventional format.

Visiting card (above)
This visiting card reads Wilhelm, Deutscher Kaiser u. König von Preußen (William, German Emperor and King of Prussia).

Business cards evolved from a fusion of traditional trade cards and visiting cards. The standard size specified by ISO 7810 ID-1 is the same as used for credit cards, 85.60 x 55mm, but the A8 paper size is also used (74 x 52mm). In the USA, the common business card size is 3.5 x 2 inches (89 x 51mm), while Japan employs the Yong size (91 x 55mm).

85.60 x 55mm

ID-1

89 x 51mm

United States

Business cards (above, left and below)
Pictured are illustrations of various standard business card sizes from around the world. With the exception of the A8 format, they are generally much wider than they are tall. Notice how the ISO standard ID-1 has the same dimensions as a credit card (above).

When specifying business card print jobs the following colour notation is used: **4/0** for a full-colour front with no back printing, **4/1** for a full-colour front with black-and-white back, and **4/4** for a full-colour front with a full-colour back.

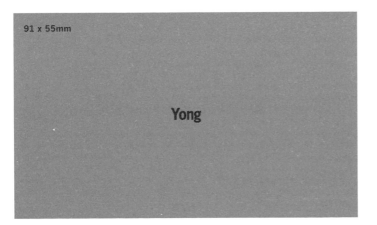

91 x 55mm

Yong

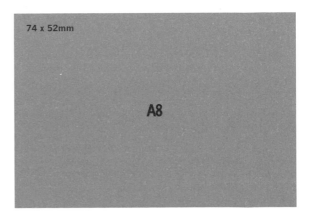

74 x 52mm

A8

6.7 Conclusion

This book has built upon a basic understanding of layout within the graphic design discipline to deepen knowledge of key concepts and methods. By developing an appreciation of the use of standards, grids and other systems to assist the positioning of elements within a design, it has aimed to better equip a graphic designer with the tools needed to produce effective designs in a timely and efficient manner, while providing ample space for creativity through the use and manipulation of these concepts.

Many of the principles presented in this volume have been illustrated with examples produced by leading contemporary graphic design studios for commercial clients. We hope that these examples provide inspiration and we would like to thank everyone who has contributed work to help enrich *The Layout Book*.

3 Deep Design	www.3deep.com.au
Blast	www.blast.co.uk
Cartlidge Levene	www.cartlidgelevene.co.uk
Faydherbe/De Vringer	www.ben-wout.nl
Fl@33	www.flat33.com
Frost Design	www.frostdesign.com.au
Gavin Ambrose	www.gavinambrose.co.uk
NB: Studio	www.nbstudio.co.uk
Peter and Paul	www.peterandpaul.co.uk
Research Studios	www.researchstudios.com
SEA Design	www.seadesign.co.uk
Spin	www.spin.co.uk
Studio Myerscough	www.studiomyerscough.com
Studio Output	www.studio-output.com
The Vast Agency	www.thevastagency.com
Third Eye Design	www.thirdeyedesign.co.uk
Thirteen	www.thirteen.co.uk
Thomas Manss & Co.	www.manss.com
Tilt	www.tiltdesign.co.uk
Untitled Design	www.untitledstudio.com
Why Not Associates	www.whynotassociates.com

Hound Dog (right)

Pictured is the cover of *Hound Dog*, a book by photographer Maarten Wetsema, created by Wout de Vringer of Faydherbe/De Vringer design studio. The book features photographs of pets in sterile, clinical interiors presented in a spacious and unassuming layout, which allows the viewer to give full attention to the images. Another spread from this publication is shown on page 86.

6.8 Glossary

Layout uses many technical terms that help designers, printers, clients and others involved in the production process accurately specify and communicate their thoughts and ideas about a job. This glossary will define some of the most common technical terms used in layout design.

Absolute measurement
A measurement of a fixed value, e.g. an inch.

Alignment
The vertical and horizontal position of type within a text block.

Appropriation
Taking the style of one discipline or item and applying it to another.

Art deco
Design style celebrating the rise of technology.

Asymmetrical grid
The same layout used on both recto and verso pages.

Balance
Visual equilibrium in a design.

Baseline grid
Series of horizontal lines for positioning design elements.

Bauhaus
German art and design school (1919–1933) that focused on functionality rather than adornment, through use of geometric forms.

Broadside
Text rotated 90 degrees to the spine to read vertically.

Canons
General principles guiding design choices.

Classical principles
Ideals about proportion and style originating in ancient Greece.

CMYK
Cyan (C), magenta (M), yellow (Y) and black (K) are the subtractive primary inks, which are combined to reproduce the red, green and blue additive primaries in the four-colour printing process.

Colour
Page element density that provides colouration.

Columns
Vertical divisions of a layout into which text is flowed.

Deconstructionism
A postmodernist approach that undermines the frame of reference and assumptions behind a pattern of thought.

Diptych
Juxtaposition of two images as part of a whole.

Dual narrative
Where two narratives or themes are present in a design.

Fields
Discrete areas within a layout for text or image placement.

Golden ratio
A division in the ratio 8:13 that produces harmonious proportions.

Grid
A guide for positioning elements.

Gutter
The centre alleyway where two pages meet at the spine. Also the space separating columns.

Indentation
A space inserted into a text block to give a starting point.

Interior design
Interior space experience formation through use of surface and spatial volume.

Juxtaposition
Side-by-side image placement to create a relationship between the images.

Layout
The placement of text and images to create the appearance of a page.

Leading
Space inserted between lines of text.

Matrices
Different structures used to divide a page and guide element placement.

Module
See Fields.

Narrative
The meaning of visual communication.

Order
One of several styles prevalent in ancient Greek architecture.

Overprinting
Where one ink is printed over another to add texture and create new colours.

Pace
Momentum or flow of a publication's content.

Passepartout
A frame or border around an image or element.

Picture boxes
Spaces created in a layout for the placement of images.

Pixel
A screen picture element that can be used as a very fine grid.

Pluralism
The use of multiple narratives.

Point size
Font size in points.

Recto/verso
The pages of an open book with recto being the right-hand page and verso the left hand.

Relative measurement
Measurement relative to the size of the type set.

Renaissance
Revival of classical concepts of art and beauty in 14th–16th-century Europe.

RGB
Red (R), green (G) and blue (B) are the additive primaries of light that produce white light when combined. In four-colour printing the additive primaries are reproduced using the subtractive primaries CMYK.

Roman road
A string of sequential images.

Symmetrical grid
A layout mirrored on the recto and verso pages.

Thumbnails
Smaller versions of a publication's spreads giving an overview of its pace.

Triptych
Juxtaposition of three images.

Typeface
The characters of a type design.

Vista
A view, scene or prospect.

White space
The empty, unprinted and unused spaces.

Druk 5 (above)
This is a spread from *Druk 5* magazine, created by
Faydherbe/De Vringer design studio, which features
photographs of roads presented in a grid with
overprinted text that acts like a centre line.

This index is intended to provide a ready reference to the various concepts, ideas and methods about the use of layout in graphic design that are contained within this volume.

6.10 Acknowledgements

We would like to thank everyone who supported us during the production of this book including the many art directors, designers and creatives who showed great generosity in allowing us to reproduce their work.

Special thanks to everyone that hunted for, collated, compiled and rediscovered some of the examples of work contained in this book. A final thank you is due to Caroline Walmsley, Brian Morris, Natalia Price-Cabrera and Sanaz Nazemi at AVA Publishing who never tired of our requests, enquiries and questions, and supported us throughout this project.

All clockwise from top left
002 Xavier Young / 004 Xavier Young / 006 Christa DeRidder, Ian Bracegirdle, Randy Plemel, Nicholas Belton / 011 photodisc / 012 Karim Hesham (pyramids image) / 013 Dover Press (bottom right) / 014 Elnur Amikishiyev / 016 Diamond Sutra © The British Library Board. All Rights Reserved / 019 Jim Tardio (Santa Maria del Fiore image) / 020 Credit: The 'Kelmscott Chaucer', published 1896 by the Kelmscott Press © Cheltenham Art Gallery & Museums, Gloucestershire, UK/The Bridgeman Art Library. Nationality/copyright status: copyright unknown / 020 Ross Thomson (stairs image) / 021 Casa Batlló, Barcelona, rubiphoto / 022 Credit: Collage M2 439, 1922 by Schwitters, Kurt (1887–1948) © Marlborough Fine Arts, London, UK/The Bridgeman Art Library. Nationality/copyright status: German/in copyright until 2019 / 023 Credit: Cover Illustration for 'Vogue' magazine, November 1926 (colour litho) by French School, (20th century) © Bibliotheque des Arts Decoratifs, Paris, France/Archives Charmet/The Bridgeman Art Library. Nationality/copyright status: French/UNDETCOP / 025 www.istockphoto.com, Niko Vujevic, Simon Detjen Schmidt / 038 Don Saunderson, Gord Horne, Dainis Derics / 046 Christophe Jacquet / 049 www.istockphoto.com / 053 Richard Simpkins / 055 photodisc / 056 photodisc (bottom two images) / 060 David Mathies / 062 Stephen Finn, Randy Plemel / 064 Xavier Young / 068 Teun van den Dries / 072 www.istockphoto.com / 075 Credit: Sketch for the original map of the London Underground, 1933 (pen & coloured ink on paper) by Beck, Harry (1903–74) © Victoria & Albert Museum, London, UK/The Stapleton Collection/The Bridgeman Art Library. Nationality/copyright status: English/in copyright until 2045 / 080 Xavier Young / 086 Xavier Young, Stanislav Khrapov / 087 Credit: Res 4720 The letter 'A', illustration for 'De Divina Proportione' by Luca Pacioli (1445–1517) 1509 (lithograph) by Vinci, Leonardo da (1452–1519) © Bibliotheque Mazarine, Paris, France/Archives Charmet/The Bridgeman Art Library. Nationality/copyright status: Italian/out of copyright / 088 Xavier Young / 089 photodisc / 096 Xavier Young / 098 Andi Berger / 100 Xavier Young / 103 Ben Heyes / 104 Xavier Young / 105 Xavier Young / 112 Xavier Young (top image) / 117 Xavier Young / 126 Credit: 'The Rite of Spring', original score by Igor Stravinsky (1882–1971), 1913 © Private Collection/The Bridgeman Art Library. Nationality/copyright status: copyright unknown / 129 Armchair=Table © Tomoko Azumi / 130 Jim Tardio / 130, 131 Max Alexander (bottom images) / 134 Xavier Young / 138 Xavier Young / 150 photodisc / 151 Timothy Ball / 152 Dušan Jankovic / 154, 155 Photography by Richard Learoyd, Marcus Ginns and Cartlidge Levene.

All reasonable attempts have been made to trace, clear and credit the copyright holders of the images reproduced in this book. However, if any credits have been inadvertently omitted, the publisher will endeavour to incorporate amendments in future editions.